WITH WORKBOOK

TOP NOTCH

English for Today's World

1A

WITH WORKBOOK

TOP NOTCH

English for Today's World

1A

Joan Saslow ■ Allen Ascher

With *Top Notch Pop Songs and Karaoke*
by Rob Morsberger

PEARSON
Longman

Top Notch: English for Today's World   1A with Workbook

Pearson Education, 10 Bank Street, White Plains, NY 10606

Editorial director: Pamela Fishman
Senior development editor: Peter Benson
Assistant development editor: Siobhan Sullivan
Vice president, director of design and production: Rhea Banker
Director of electronic production: Aliza Greenblatt
Managing editor: Mike Kemper
Production editor: Full-service production provided by Camelot Editorial Services
Art director: Ann France
Senior manufacturing buyer: Dave Dickey
Photo research: Aerin Csigay
Digital layout specialist: Warren Fischbach
Text composition: Studio Montage, Word & Image Design Studio, Inc.
Text font: Palatino 11/13, Frutiger 10/12

ISBNs: 0-13-110413-6 (Student's Book with Workbook and Audio CD)
    0-13-238702-6 (Student's Book with Workbook and Take-Home Super CD-ROM)

Printed in the United States of America
10–QWE–10 09

ntents

RENCE SECTION FOR 1A AND 1B

ose Luis Pelaez, In
rbis; p. 9 (left) Ton
lams/Hansen Photo
(father-in-law) Jame
Edit; p. 31 (middle
phy LLC; p. 33 (do
Yang Liu/Corbis; p
aguez/Globe Photo
Inc., (Carys Dough
an McVay/Getty In
y Meshkinyar/Get
rm) Zhenjiang San
rian Hagiwara/Pict
lia Library, (Ice cre
etty Images; p. w
niddle right) Tim
Images, (Jane) Cle

6 Dorling Kindersl
pier) Getty Images

3, W31; Scott Fray
; 49, 58; NSV Prod
48.

BOOK

Scope and Sequence for 1A and 1B

GRAMMAR BOOSTER

UNIT	Vocabulary*	Conversation Strategies	Grammar	
1 Getting Acquainted Page 4	• Titles • Occupations • Nationalities	• Use <u>As a matter of fact</u> to introduce surprising information • Begin responses with a question to clarify • Provide information beyond <u>Yes</u> or <u>No</u> when answering a question	• The verb <u>be</u>: <u>Yes</u> / <u>no</u> questions Contractions Information questions • Possessive nouns and adjectives	• Further explanation of usage and form: <u>be</u> • Further explanation of form: possessive adjectives
2 Going Out Page 16 *Top Notch* Song: "Going Out"	• Entertainment events • Kinds of music • Locations and directions	• Use <u>Really?</u> to show enthusiasm • Use <u>I'd love to</u> to accept an invitation • Use <u>I'd love to, but...</u> or <u>Thanks, but...</u> to decline • Use <u>Excuse me</u> to approach a stranger	• The verb <u>be</u>: Questions with <u>When</u>, <u>What time</u>, and <u>Where</u> Contractions • Prepositions of time and place: <u>On</u>, <u>in</u>, <u>at</u>	• Further explanation of usage: prepositions of time and place
3 Talking about Families Page 28	• Family relationships • Ways to describe similarities and differences • Marital status and relationships	• Start answers with <u>Well</u> to give oneself time to think • Use <u>That's great!</u> to show enthusiasm • Ask follow-up questions to keep a conversation going • Initiate polite conversation with <u>So</u>	• The simple present tense: Statements <u>Yes</u> / <u>no</u> questions Information questions	• Further explanation of usage and form: the simple present tense
4 Coping with Technology Page 40	• Descriptive adjectives • Electronics • Ways to sympathize • Machines at home and at work • Machine features • Ways to state a complaint	• Use <u>How's it going?</u> and <u>Hey</u> to greet someone informally • Use word stress to clarify meaning • Use <u>What about...?</u> to make a suggestion • Use <u>Really?</u> to ask for confirmation • Use <u>Hello?</u> to answer the telephone	• The present continuous: for actions in progress and the future	• Spelling rules for the present participle • Further explanation of form: the present continuous
5 Eating in, Eating out Page 52 *Top Notch* Song: "The World Cafe"	• Menu items • Categories of food • What to say to a waiter or waitress • Food and health	• Use <u>I think I'll have</u> to soften food orders • Use <u>Good idea!</u> to accept a suggestion enthusiastically	• Count and non-count nouns / <u>there is</u> and <u>there are</u> • <u>A</u>, <u>an</u>, <u>the</u>	• Categories of non-count nouns • Verb agreement: non-count nouns • Expressing quantities: non-count nouns • <u>How much</u> / <u>How many</u> • Spelling rules: plural nouns • <u>Some</u> / <u>any</u>

*In *Top Notch*, the term *vocabulary* refers to individual words, phrases, and expressions.

Speaking	Pronunciation	Listening	Reading	Writing
• Exchange personal information • Clarify and confirm information • Offer to introduce someone • Introduce someone • Shift to informality	• Rising and falling intonation for questions	• Conversations about people Task: listen for names, occupations, and nationalities	• Short introductions of people who travel for their jobs • Student descriptions	• Introduce a classmate • Introduce yourself
• Offer, accept, and decline invitations • Ask and answer questions about events • Ask for and give directions • Talk about music likes and dislikes	• Repetition to confirm information	• Invitations to events Task: identify the events and times • Phone calls to a box office Task: identify events, times, and ticket prices	• Newspaper entertainment listings • Arts festival website • People's descriptions of their musical tastes • Music survey	• Describe your own musical tastes
• Identify family relationships • Ask about and describe family members • Compare people • Discuss family size	• Blending sounds: <u>Does</u> + <u>he</u> / <u>Does</u> + <u>she</u>	• Descriptions of family members Task: listen for people's marital status or relationship • An interview about a brother Task: determine similarities and differences • Descriptions of families Task: determine size of family and number of children	• Article about different family sizes • Article comparing a brother and sister	• Compare two people in your own family • Compare two siblings in another family
• Ask for and make suggestions • Offer reasons for purchasing a product • Express frustration and offer sympathy • Describe features of machines • Complain when things don't work	• Rising and falling intonation for questions: review	• Complaints about machines Task: identify the machines • Radio advertisements Task: listen for adjectives that describe machines • Complaints to a hotel front desk Task: identify the problem and room number • Problems with machines Task: write the problem	• Ads from electronics catalogs	• Describe one of your own machines • Describe all the problems in a picture
• Discuss what to eat • Order, get the check, and pay for a meal • Describe your own diet • Discuss food and health choices	• Pronunciation of <u>the</u> before consonant and vowel sounds	• Conversations about food Task: listen for and classify food items • Conversations in a restaurant Task: predict a diner's next statement • Conversations while eating Task: determine the location of the conversation	• Menus • Nutrition website	• Describe a traditional food in your own country • Write a story based on a picture

UNIT	Vocabulary	Conversation Strategies	Grammar	
6 **Staying in Shape** *Page 64* *Top Notch* Song: "A Typical Day"	• Physical and everyday activities • Places for sports and games • Talking about health habits	• Use <u>Sorry, I can't</u> to decline regretfully • Provide an explanation for declining an invitation • Use <u>Actually</u> to introduce contrast	• <u>Can</u> and <u>have to</u> • The simple present tense and the present continuous • Frequency adverbs • Time expressions	• Further explanation of form: <u>can</u> / <u>have to</u> • Non-action verbs • Further explanation of usage and form: frequency adverbs / time expressions
7 **Finding Something to Wear** *Page 76*	• Categories of clothing • Clothing described as "pairs" • Types of clothing and shoes • Interior locations and directions • Describing clothes	• Use <u>Excuse me</u> to indicate that you need assistance in a store • Use <u>Excuse me?</u> when you don't understand or didn't hear	• Comparative adjectives • Object pronouns: as direct objects and in prepositional phrases	• Further explanation of spelling and usage: comparative adjectives • Further explanation of usage: direct and indirect objects
8 **Getting Away** *Page 88* *Top Notch* Song: "My Dream Vacation"	• Types of vacations • Adjectives for travel conditions • Adjectives to describe vacations • Travel problems	• Use <u>actually</u> to acknowledge another's interest • Say <u>I'm fine</u> to decline assistance • After answering a question, ask <u>What about you?</u> to show reciprocal interest	• The past tense of <u>be</u> • The simple past tense: regular and irregular verbs	• Further explanation of usage and form: the past tense of <u>be</u> • Further explanation of usage and form: the simple past tense • Spelling rules: regular verbs in the simple past tense
9 **Taking Transportation** *Page 100*	• Tickets and trips • Travel services • Airline passenger information • Means of transportation • Transportation problems	• Say <u>Oh no</u> to indicate dismay • Say <u>Let me check</u> to buy time to find the answer to a question	• <u>Could</u> and <u>should</u> • <u>Be going to</u> for the future	• Further explanation of meaning: <u>can</u>, <u>should</u>, <u>could</u> • Explanation of form: modals • Comparison of ways to express the future
10 **Shopping Smart** *Page 112* *Top Notch* Song: "Shopping for Souvenirs"	• Money and travel • Electronic products • Handicrafts • Talking about prices	• Use <u>can</u> to indicate willingness to bargain • Use demonstratives to clarify intention	• Superlative adjectives • <u>Too</u> and <u>enough</u>	• Contrasting the comparative and the superlative • Spelling rules for superlatives • Intensifiers <u>too</u>, <u>really</u>, and <u>very</u>

Speaking	Pronunciation	Listening	Reading	Writing
• Suggest and plan an activity • Provide an excuse • Ask about and describe daily routines • Discuss exercise and diet	• <u>Can</u> / <u>can't</u> • Third-person singular endings	• Conversations about immediate plans <u>Task</u>: identify destinations • Descriptions of exercise and diet routines <u>Task</u>: identify each person's health habits • Conversations about diet and exercise <u>Task</u>: complete the statement	• Graph showing calories burned by activity • Health survey • Article about Brooke Ellison's daily schedule	• Report about a classmate's typical day • Recount your own typical day
• Discuss where you shop • Ask a clerk for help • Shop and pay for clothes • Ask for and give directions within a building • Discuss culturally appropriate dress	• Contrastive stress for clarification	• Conversations about clothing needs <u>Task</u>: choose the clothing item • Directions in a store <u>Task</u>: mark the store departments • Conversations about clothes <u>Task</u>: determine the location of the conversation	• Clothing store website • Article about clothing tips for travelers • Personal dress code survey	• Give advice about clothing for visitors to your country • Plan clothing for a trip and explain reasons
• Greet someone arriving from a trip • Describe travel conditions • Talk about leisure activities • Discuss vacation preferences • Complain about travel problems	• Simple past-tense endings	• Descriptions of vacations <u>Task</u>: identify the vacation problems • Descriptions of travel experiences <u>Task</u>: choose the correct adjective	• Vacation ads • Travel agency brochure • Vacation survey • Student articles about vacations	• Describe a past vacation • Describe another person's vacation
• Discuss schedules and buy tickets • Ask for and give advice • Book travel services • Discuss travel plans • Describe transportation problems	• Intonation of alternatives	• Requests for travel services <u>Task</u>: identify the service requested • Airport announcements <u>Task</u>: listen for delays and cancellations • Conversations about transportation problems <u>Task</u>: complete the statement • Conversations about transportation <u>Task</u>: match the conversation with the picture	• Airport departure schedule • Travel survey • News clippings about transportation problems	• Recount transportation problems on a past trip • Imagine your next trip
• Ask for and give a recommendation • Discuss price range • Bargain for a lower price • Discuss tipping customs • Describe a shopping experience	• Rising intonation to clarify information	• Recommendations of electronic products <u>Task</u>: identify the product • Shopping stories <u>Task</u>: listen for products and prices • Conversations about electronics purchases <u>Task</u>: check satisfactory or not satisfactory to the customer	• Travel guide about money and shopping • Article about tipping customs • Tipping survey • Story about a shopping experience	• Narrate a true story about a shopping experience • Create a shopping guide for your city

Acknowledgments

Top Notch International Advisory Board

The authors gratefully acknowledge the substantive and formative contributions of the members of the International Advisory Board.

CHERYL BELL, Middlesex County College, Middlesex, New Jersey, USA • **ELMA CABAHUG**, City College of San Francisco, San Francisco, California, USA • **JO CARAGATA**, Mukogawa Women's University, Hyogo, Japan • **ANN CARTIER**, Palo Alto Adult School, Palo Alto, California, USA • **TERRENCE FELLNER**, Himeji Dokkyo University, Hyogo, Japan • **JOHN FUJIMORI**, Meiji Gakuin High School, Tokyo, Japan • **ARETA ULHANA GALAT**, Escola Superior de Estudos Empresariais e Informática, Curitiba, Brazil • **DOREEN M. GAYLORD**, Kanazawa Technical College, Ishikawa, Japan • **EMILY GEHRMAN**, Newton International College, Garden Grove, California, USA • **ANN-MARIE HADZIMA**, National Taiwan University, Taipei, Taiwan • **KAREN KYONG-AI PARK**, Seoul National University, Seoul, Korea • **ANA PATRICIA MARTÍNEZ VITE DIP. R.S.A.**, Universidad del Valle de México, Mexico City, Mexico • **MICHELLE ANN MERRITT, PROULEX/** Universidad de Guadalajara, Guadalajara, Mexico • **ADRIANNE P. OCHOA**, Georgia State University, Atlanta, Georgia, USA • **LOUIS PARDILLO**, Korea Herald English Institute, Seoul, Korea • **THELMA PERES**, Casa Thomas Jefferson, Brasilia, Brazil • **DIANNE RUGGIERO**, Broward Community College, Davie, Florida, USA • **KEN SCHMIDT**, Tohoku Fukushi University, Sendai, Japan • **ALISA A. TAKEUCHI**, Garden Grove Adult Education, Garden Grove, California, USA • **JOSEPHINE TAYLOR**, Centro Colombo Americano, Bogotá, Colombia • **PATRICIA VECIÑO**, Instituto Cultural Argentino Norteamericano, Buenos Aires, Argentina • **FRANCES WESTBROOK**, AUA Language Center, Bangkok, Thailand

Reviewers and Piloters

Many thanks also to the reviewers and piloters all over the world who reviewed *Top Notch* in its final form.

G. Julian Abaqueta, Huachiew Chalermprakiet University, Samutprakarn, Thailand • **David Aline**, Kanagawa University, Kanagawa, Japan • **Marcia Alves**, Centro Cultural Brasil Estados Unidos, Franca, Brazil • **Yousef Al-Yacoub**, Qatar Petroleum, Doha, Qatar • **Maristela Barbosa Silveira e Silva**, Instituto Cultural Brasil-Estados Unidos, Manaus, Brazil • **Beth Bartlett**, Centro Colombo Americano, Cali, Colombia • **Carla Battigelli**, University of Zulia, Maracaibo, Venezuela • **Claudia Bautista**, C.B.C., Caracas, Venezuela • **Rob Bell**, Shumei Yachiyo High School, Chiba, Japan • **Dr. Maher Ben Moussa**, Sharjah University, Sharjah, United Arab Emirates • **Elaine Cantor**, Englewood Senior High School, Jacksonville, Florida, USA • **María Aparecida Capellari**, SENAC, São Paulo, Brazil • **Eunice Carrillo Ramos**, Colegio Durango, Naucalpan, Mexico • **Janette Carvalhinho de Oliveira**, Centro de Línguas (UFES), Vitória, Brazil • **María Amelia Carvalho Fonseca**, Centro Cultural Brasil-Estados Unidos, Belém, Brazil • **Audy Castañeda**, Instituto Pedagógico de Caracas, Caracas, Venezuela • **Ching-Fen Chang**, National Chiao Tung University, Hsinchu, Taiwan • **Ying-Yu Chen**, Chinese Culture University, Taipei, Taiwan • **Joyce Chin**, The Language Training and Testing Center, Taipei, Taiwan • **Eun Cho**, Pagoda Language School, Seoul, Korea • **Hyungzung Cho**, MBC Language Institute, Seoul, Korea • **Dong Sua Choi**, MBC Language Institute, Seoul, Korea • **Jeong Mi Choi**, Freelancer, Seoul, Korea • **Peter Chun**, Pagoda Language School, Seoul, Korea • **Eduardo Corbo**, Legacy ELT, Salto, Uruguay • **Marie Cosgrove**, Surugadai University, Saitama, Japan • **María Antonieta Covarrubias Souza**, Centro Escolar Akela, Mexico City, Mexico • **Katy Cox**, Casa Thomas Jefferson, Brasilia, Brazil • **Michael Donovan**, Gakushuin University, Tokyo, Japan • **Stewart Dorward**, Shumei Eiko High School, Saitama, Japan • **Ney Eric Espina**, Centro Venezolano Americano del Zulia, Maracaibo, Venezuela • **Edith Espino**, Centro Especializado de Lenguas - Universidad Tecnológica de Panamá, El Dorado, Panama • **Allen P. Fermon**, Instituto Brasil-Estados Unidos, Ceará, Brazil • **Simão Ferreira Banha**, Phil Young's English School, Curitiba, Brazil • **María Elena Flores Lara**, Colegio Mercedes, Mexico City, Mexico • **Valesca Fróis Nassif**, Associação Cultural Brasil-Estados Unidos, Salvador, Brazil • **José Fuentes**, Empire Language Consulting, Caracas, Venezuela • **José Luis Guerrero**, Colegio Cristóbal Colón, Mexico City, Mexico • **Claudia Patricia Gutiérrez**, Centro Colombo Americano, Cali, Colombia • **Valerie Hansford**, Asia University, Tokyo, Japan • **Gene Hardstark**, Dotkyo University, Saitama, Japan • **Maiko Hata**, Kansai University, Osaka, Japan • **Susan Elizabeth Haydock Miranda de Araujo**, Centro Cultural Brasil Estados Unidos, Belém, Brazil • **Gabriela Herrera**, Fundametal, Valencia, Venezuela • **Sandy Ho**, GEOS International, New York, New York, USA • **Yuri Hosoda**, Showa Women's University, Tokyo, Japan • **Hsiao-I Hou**, Shu-Te University, Kaohsiung County, Taiwan • **Kuei-ping Hsu**, National Tsing Hua University, Hsinchu, Taiwan • **Chia-yu Huang**, National Tsing Hua University, Hsinchu, Taiwan • **Caroline C. Hwang**, National Taipei University of Science and Technology, Taipei, Taiwan • **Diana Jones**, Angloamericano, Mexico City, Mexico • **Eunjeong Kim**, Freelancer, Seoul, Korea • **Julian Charles King**, Qatar Petroleum, Doha, Qatar • **Bruce Lee**, CIE: Foreign Language Institute, Seoul, Korea • **Myunghee Lee**, MBC Language Institute, Seoul, Korea • **Naidnapa Leoprasertkul**, Language Development Center, Mahasarakham University, Mahasarakham, Thailand • **Eleanor S. Leu**, Souchow University, Taipei, Taiwan • **Eliza Liu**, Chinese Culture University, Taipei, Taiwan • **Carlos Lizárraga**, Angloamericano, Mexico City, Mexico • **Philippe Loussarevian**, Keio University Shonan Fujisawa High School, Kanagawa, Japan • **Jonathan Lynch**, Azabu University, Tokyo, Japan • **Thomas Mach**, Konan University, Hyogo, Japan • **Lilian Mandel Civatti**, Associação Cultural Brasil-Estados Unidos, Salvador, Brazil • **Hakan Mansuroglu**, Zoni Language Center, West New York, New Jersey, USA • **Martha McGaughey**, Language Training Institute, Englewood Cliffs, New Jersey, USA • **David Mendoza Plascencia**, Instituto Internacional de Idiomas, Naucalpan, Mexico • **Theresa Mezo**, Interamerican University, Río Piedras, Puerto Rico • **Luz Adriana Montenegro Silva**, Colegio CAFAM, Bogotá, Colombia • **Magali de Moraes Menti**, Instituto Lingua, Porto Alegre, Brazil • **Massoud Moslehpour**, The Overseas Chinese Institute of Technology, Taichung, Taiwan • **Jennifer Nam**, IKE, Seoul, Korea • **Marcos Norelle F. Victor**, Instituto Brasil-Estados Unidos, Ceará, Brazil • **Luz María Olvera**, Instituto Juventud del Estado de México, Naucalpan, Mexico • **Roxana Orrego Ramírez**, Universidad Diego Portales, Santiago, Chile • **Ming-Jong Pan**, National Central University, Jhongli City, Taiwan • **Sandy Park**, Topia Language School, Seoul, Korea • **Patrícia Elizabeth Peres Martins**, Instituto Brasil-Estados Unidos, Rio de Janeiro, Brazil • **Rodrigo Peza**, Passport Language Centers, Bogotá, Colombia • **William Porter**, Osaka Institute of Technology, Osaka, Japan • **Caleb Prichard**, Kwansei Gakuin University, Hyogo, Japan • **Mirna Quintero**, Instituto Pedagógico de Caracas, Caracas, Venezuela • **Roberto Rabbini**, Seigakuin University, Saitama, Japan • **Terri Rapoport**, Berkeley College, White Plains, New York, USA • **Yvette Rieser**, Centro Electrónico de Idiomas, Maracaibo, Venezuela • **Orlando Rodríguez**, New English Teaching School, Paysandu, Uruguay • **Mayra Rosario**, Pontificia Universidad Católica Madre y Maestra, Santiago, Dominican Republic • **Peter Scout**, Sakura no Seibo Junior College, Fukushima, Japan • **Jungyeon Shim**, EG School, Seoul, Korea • **Keum Ok Song**, MBC Language Institute, Seoul, Korea • **Assistant Professor Dr. Reongrudee Soonthornmanee**, Chulalongkorn University Language Institute, Bangkok, Thailand • **Claudia Stanisclause**, The Language College, Maracay, Venezuela • **Tom Suh**, The Princeton Review, Seoul, Korea • **Phiphawin Suphawat**, KhonKaen University, KhonKaen, Thailand • **Craig Sweet**, Poole Gakuin Junior and Senior High Schools, Osaka, Japan • **Yi-nien Josephine Twu**, National Tsing Hua University, Hsinchu, Taiwan • **Maria Christina Uchôa Close**, Instituto Cultural Brasil-Estados Unidos, São José dos Campos, Brazil • **Luz Vanegas Lopera**, Lexicom The Place For Learning English, Medellín, Colombia • **Julieta Vasconcelos García**, Centro Escolar del Lago, A.C., Mexico City, Mexico • **Carol Vaughan**, Kanto Kokusai High School, Tokyo, Japan • **Patricia Celia Veciño**, Instituto Cultural Argentino Norteamericano, Buenos Aires, Argentina • **Isabela Villas Boas**, Casa Thomas Jefferson, Brasilia, Brazil • **Iole Vitti**, Peanuts English School, Poços de Caldas, Brazil • **Gabi Witthaus**, Qatar Petroleum, Doha, Qatar • **Yi-Ling Wu**, Shih Chien University, Taipei, Taiwan • **Chad Wynne**, Osaka Keizai University, Osaka, Japan • **Belkis Yanes**, Freelance Instructor, Caracas, Venezuela • **I-Chieh Yang**, Chung-kuo Institute of Technology, Taipei, Taiwan • **Emil Ysona**, Instituto Cultural Dominico-Americano, Santo Domingo, Dominican Republic • **Chi-fang Yu**, Soo Chow University, Taipei, Taiwan, • **Shigeki Yusa**, Sendai Shirayuri Women's College, Sendai, Japan

To the Teacher

What is Top Notch?

- *Top Notch* is a six-level communicative English course for adults and young adults, with two beginning entry levels.
- *Top Notch* prepares students to interact successfully and confidently with both native and non-native speakers of English.
- *Top Notch* demonstrably brings students to a "Top Notch" level of communicative competence.

Key Elements of the Top Notch Instructional Design

Concise two-page lessons

Each easy-to-teach two-page lesson is designed for one class session and begins with a clearly stated communication goal and ends with controlled or free communication practice. Each lesson provides vocabulary, grammar, and social language contextualized in all four skills, keeping the pace of a class session lively and varied.

Daily confirmation of progress

Adult and young adult students need to observe and confirm their own progress. In *Top Notch*, students conclude each class session with a controlled or free practice activity that demonstrates their ability to use new vocabulary, grammar, and social language. This motivates and keeps students eager to continue their study of English and builds their pride in being able to speak accurately, fluently, and authentically.

Real language

Carefully exposing students to authentic, natural English, both receptively and productively, is a necessary component of building understanding and expression. All conversation models feature the language people really use; nowhere to be found is "textbook English" written merely to exemplify grammar.

Practical content

In addition to classic topical vocabulary, grammar, and conversation, *Top Notch* includes systematic practice of highly practical language, such as: how to ask for a restaurant check, how to ask whether the tip is included in the bill, how to complain when the air-conditioning in a hotel room doesn't work, how to bargain for a lower price—usable language today's students want and need.

Memorable model conversations

Effective language instruction must make language memorable. The full range of social and functional communicative needs is presented through practical model conversations that are intensively practiced and manipulated, first within a guided model and then in freer and more personalized formats.

High-impact vocabulary syllabus

In order to ensure students' solid acquisition of vocabulary essential for communication, *Top Notch* contains explicit presentation, practice, and systematic extended recycling of words, collocations, and expressions appropriate at each level of study. The extensive captioned illustrations, photos, definitions, examples, and contextualized sentences remove doubts about meaning and provide a permanent in-book reference for student test preparation. An added benefit is that teachers don't have to search for pictures to bring to class and don't have to resort to translating vocabulary into the students' native language.

Learner-supportive grammar

Grammar is approached explicitly and cognitively, through form, meaning, and use—both within the Student's Book units and in a bound-in Grammar Booster. Charts provide examples and paradigms enhanced by simple usage notes at students' level of comprehension. This takes the guesswork out of meaning, makes lesson preparation easier for teachers, and provides students with comprehensible charts for permanent reference and test preparation. All presentations of grammar are followed by exercises to ensure adequate practice.

English as an international language

Top Notch prepares students for interaction with both native and non-native speakers of English, both linguistically and culturally. English is treated as an international language, rather than the language of a particular country or region. In addition, *Top Notch* helps students develop a cultural fluency by creating an awareness of the varied rules across cultures for: politeness, greetings and introductions, appropriateness of dress in different settings, conversation do's and taboos, table manners, and other similar issues.

Two beginning-level texts

Beginning students can be placed either in *Top Notch 1* or *Top Notch Fundamentals*, depending on ability and background. Even absolute beginners can start with confidence in *Top Notch Fundamentals*. False beginners can begin with *Top Notch 1*. The *Top Notch Placement Test* clarifies the best placement within the series.

Estimated teaching time

Each level of *Top Notch* is designed for 60 to 90 instructional hours and contains a full range of supplementary components and enrichment devices to tailor the course to individual needs.

Components of *Top Notch 1*

Student's Book with Take-Home Super CD-ROM

The Super CD-ROM includes a variety of exciting interactive activities: Speaking Practice, Interactive Workbook, Games and Puzzles, and *Top Notch Pop* Karaoke. The disk can also be played on an audio CD player to listen to the Conversation Models and the *Top Notch Pop* songs.

Teacher's Edition with Daily Lesson Plans

Complete yet concise lesson plans are provided for each class. Corpus notes provide essential information from the *Longman Spoken American Corpus* and the *Longman Learner's Corpus*. In addition, a free Teacher's Resource Disk offers the following printable extension activpities to personalize your teaching style:

- Grammar self-checks
- *Top Notch Pop* song activities
- Writing process worksheets
- Learning strategies
- Pronunciation activities and supplements
- Extra reading comprehension activities
- Vocabulary cards and cumulative vocabulary activities
- Graphic organizers
- Pair work cards

Copy & Go: Ready-made Interactive Activities for Busy Teachers

Interactive games, puzzles, and other practice activities in convenient photocopiable form support the Student's Book content and provide a welcome change of pace.

Complete Classroom Audio Program

The audio program, available in cassette or audio CD format, contains listening comprehension activities, rhythm and intonation practice, and targeted pronunciation activities that focus on accurate and comprehensible pronunciation.

Because *Top Notch* prepares students for international communication, a variety of native and non-native speakers are included to ready students for the world outside the classroom. The audio program also includes the five *Top Notch Pop* songs in standard and karaoke form.

Workbook

A tightly linked illustrated Workbook contains exercises that provide additional practice and reinforcement of language concepts and skills from *Top Notch* and its Grammar Booster.

Complete Assessment Package with *ExamView®* Software

Ten easy-to-administer and easy-to-score unit achievement tests assess listening, vocabulary, grammar, social language, reading, and writing. Two review tests, one mid-book and one end-of-book, provide additional cumulative assessment. Two speaking tests assess progress in speaking. In addition to the photocopiable achievement tests, *ExamView®* software enables teachers to tailor-make tests to best meet their needs by combining items in any way they wish.

Top Notch TV

A lively and entertaining video offers a TV-style situation comedy that reintroduces language from each *Top Notch* unit, plus authentic unrehearsed interviews with English speakers from around the world and authentic karaoke. Packaged with the video are activity worksheets and a booklet with teaching suggestions and complete video scripts.

Companion Website

A Companion Website at www.longman.com/topnotch provides numerous additional resources for students and teachers. This no-cost, high-benefit feature includes opportunities for further practice of language and content from the *Top Notch* Student's Book.

Welcome to Top Notch!

About the Authors

Joan Saslow

Joan Saslow has taught English as a Foreign Language and English as a Second Language to adults and young adults in both South America and the United States. She taught English and French at the Binational Centers of Valparaíso and Viña del Mar, Chile, and the Catholic University of Valparaíso. In the United States, Ms. Saslow taught English as a Foreign Language to Japanese university students at Marymount College and to international students in Westchester Community College's intensive English program as well as workplace English at the General Motors auto assembly plant in Tarrytown, NY.

Ms. Saslow is the series director of Longman's popular five-level adult series *True Colors: An EFL Course for Real Communication* and of *True Voices*, a five-level video course. She is author of *Ready to Go: Language, Lifeskills, and Civics*, a four-level adult ESL series; *Workplace Plus*, a vocational English series; and of *Literacy Plus*, a two-level series that teaches literacy, English, and culture to adult pre-literate students. She is also author of *English in Context: Reading Comprehension for Science and Technology*, a three-level series for English for special purposes. In addition, Ms. Saslow has been an author, an editor of language teaching materials, a teacher-trainer, and a frequent speaker at gatherings of EFL and ESL teachers for over thirty years.

Allen Ascher

Allen Ascher has been a teacher and teacher-trainer in both China and the United States, as well as an administrator and a publisher. Mr. Ascher specialized in teaching listening and speaking to students at the Beijing Second Foreign Language Institute, to hotel workers at a major international hotel in China, and to Japanese students from Chubu University studying English at Ohio University. In New York, Mr. Ascher taught students of all language backgrounds and abilities at the City University of New York, and he trained teachers in the TESOL Certificate Program at the New School. He was also the academic director of the International English Language Institute at Hunter College.

Mr. Ascher has provided lively workshops for EFL teachers throughout Asia, Latin America, Europe, and the Middle East. He is author of the popular *Think about Editing: A Grammar Editing Guide for ESL Writers*. As a publisher, Mr. Ascher played a key role in the creation of some of the most widely used materials for adults, including: *True Colors, NorthStar, Focus on Grammar, Global Links*, and *Ready to Go*. Mr. Ascher has an M.A. in Applied Linguistics from Ohio University.

Welcome to *Top Notch!*

Read and listen. Then listen again and repeat in the pauses.

> Hello. My name's Peter.

> Hi. I'm Alexandra. But everyone calls me Alex.

More greetings
Good morning.
Good afternoon.
Good evening.

1. Introduce yourself.

> What do you do?

> I'm a student. And you?

> I'm a student, too.

2. Tell someone what you do.

> Alex, this is Emily. Emily, this is Alex.

> Nice to meet you, Alex.

> Nice to meet you, too.

3. Introduce someone.

> Well, it was nice meeting you.

> See you later.

> Bye.

More ways to say good-bye
Good-bye.
Take it easy.
Take care.
Good night.

4. Say good-bye.

B GROUP WORK.
Get to know your classmates.

Introduce someone to your class.

C 🎧 **Read and listen. Then listen again and repeat in the pauses.**

1.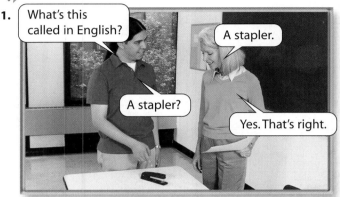

What's this called in English?

A stapler.

A stapler?

Yes. That's right.

2.

What's your last name, please?

Choi.

I'm sorry. Could you repeat that?

Sure. It's Choi.

3.

How do you say your last name?

Yuan.

Yuan? Thanks.

4.

How do you spell your first name?

G-U-Y.

Thank you.

D 🎧 **Listen to the conversations. Then listen again and write the names.**

1. _____   _____
   first name   last name

2. _____   _____
   first name   last name

E **PAIR WORK. What's this called in English? Use your dictionary.**

1. _____ **2.** _____ **3.** _____ **4.** _____

UNIT 1

Getting Acquainted

UNIT GOALS

1 Get to know someone
2 Offer to introduce someone
3 Talk about people
4 Interview a classmate

A **TOPIC PREVIEW.** Why are <u>you</u> studying English?

☐ **for business**

☐ **for travel**

☐ **for study**

☐ **to get to know people who don't speak my language**

B Enroll in *Top Notch*.

Mr. ☐	
Mrs. ☐	
Ms. ☐	Last / Family Name
Miss ☐	
	First / Given Name
	Nationality
	Occupation

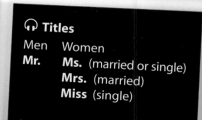

🎧 **Titles**

Men	Women
Mr.	**Ms.** (married or single)
	Mrs. (married)
	Miss (single)

Use titles with family names, NOT first or given names.

◆ C ◆ 🎧 **SOUND BITES.** Read along silently as you listen to a natural conversation.

DIANA: Mom, this is my teacher, Mr. Mills.

MRS. DARE: Nice to meet you, Mr. Mills.

MR. MILLS: Please call me Tom.

MR. MILLS: Let me introduce you to my wife, Carol.... Carol, Mrs. Dare and her daughter, Diana.

MRS. MILLS: Nice to meet you both.

◆ D ◆ **Complete each sentence.**

1. Mrs. Dare calls Diana's teacher _____.
   a. Mr. Mills   **b.** Tom   **c.** Mr. Tom

2. Mr. Mills calls his wife _____.
   a. Carol   **b.** Mrs. Mills   **c.** Ms. Carol

3. Mr. Mills calls his student _____.
   a. Ms. Dare   **b.** Diana   **c.** Miss Dare

WHAT ABOUT **YOU?**

Complete your response to each person.

1. Nice to meet you.

Josh   Groban
GIVEN NAME   FAMILY NAME
singer
OCCUPATION

Nice to meet you, _____.
a. Mr. Josh
b. Mr. Groban
c. Ms. Groban

2. Good to meet you.

Streep   Meryl
LAST NAME   FIRST NAME
actress
OCCUPATION

Good to meet you, _____.
a. Ms. Streep
b. Mr. Meryl
c. Ms. Meryl

3. Pleasure to meet you.

FAMILY NAME: Yao
FIRST NAME: Ming
OCCUPATION: basketball player

Pleasure to meet you, _____.
a. Mr. Yao
b. Mr. Ming
c. Ms. Yao

Get to Know Someone

🎧 CONVERSATION MODEL Read and listen.

A: Are you Bill?
B: No, I'm David. That's Bill over there.
A: Well, I'm Stacey. It's nice to meet you, David.
B: You, too.
A: Are you a student here?
B: As a matter of fact, I am.

🎧 Rhythm and intonation practice

A **GRAMMAR.** <u>Yes</u> / <u>no</u> questions and short answers with the verb <u>be</u>

Are you a student?	Yes, I am.	No, I'm not.
Is he married?	Yes, he is.	No, he isn't. [No, he's not.]
Is Claire from the U.S.?	Yes, she is.	No, she isn't. [No, she's not.]
Are you in my class?	Yes, we are.	No, we aren't. [No, we're not.]
Are they Canadian?	Yes, they are.	No, they aren't. [No, they're not.]
Are your friends here?	Yes, they are.	No, they aren't. [No, they're not.]

> **Contractions**
> **I'm** = I am
> **you're** = you are
> **he's** = he is
> **she's** = she is
> **we're** = we are
> **they're** = they are

GRAMMAR BOOSTER

PAGE G1
For more . . .

B Complete the questions and answers. Use contractions when possible.

_____ from China?
1.

Yes, as a matter of fact,
_____.
2.

_____ he an athlete?
3.

No, _____.
4.

_____ an artist.
5.

Oh, those are the new students. _____ 6. from Canada?

No, _____ 7. . I think _____ 8. from the U.K.

Hello. _____ 9. Nancy and Ron?

No, _____ 10. . I'm Jake and this is Patty.

C **PAIR WORK.** Write questions for your partner. Then exchange questions. Write answers to your partner's questions.

> Are you from São Paulo?

> No, I'm not. I'm from Santos.

CONVERSATION **PAIR WORK**

Write all your classmates' names on the chalkboard. Then get to know your classmates. Use the guide, or create a new conversation.

A: Are you _____?

B: _____.

A: Well, I'm _____. It's nice to meet you, _____.

B: _____ …

Continue the conversation in your <u>own</u> way.

Offer to Introduce Someone

🎧 CONVERSATION **MODEL** **Read and listen.**

A: Who's that?
B: Over there? Her name's Kate.
Come. I'll introduce you.

• • •

B: Lauren, I'd like you to
meet Kate.
A: Nice to meet you, Kate.
C: Nice to meet you, too.

🎧 **Rhythm and intonation practice**

 GRAMMAR. **Information questions with <u>be</u>**

Who's that?	That's Park Su.
Who are they?	They're my classmates.
Where's he from?	He's from Tokyo.
What's your occupation?	I'm a student.
How old are they?	He's sixteen and his brother is ten.
What's your nickname?	Everyone calls me Susie.
What are their names?	Costas and Ahmed.
What's his e-mail address?	ted@kr.com [say "ted at k r dot com"]

Possessive nouns
the **teacher's** name
Peter's address

Possessive adjectives
I = **my**   it = **its**
you = **your**   we = **our**
he = **his**   they = **their**
she = **her**

Contractions
Who's = Who is
What's = What is
Where's = Where is
That's = That is

GRAMMAR BOOSTER

PAGE G2
For more . . .

B **Complete the conversations.**
Use contractions when possible.

1. **A:** _____ that over there?
   B: Oh, that _____ Erol.
      He _____ from Turkey.
   A: _____ is he? He looks
      very young.
   B: I think he _____ twenty-five.

Istanbul, Turkey

2. A: _____ that your new neighbor?

   B: Yeah. _____ name _____ Roberta.

   A: _____ she from?

   B: Costa Rica.

Costa Rican rainforest

Mieko and Rika

3. A: _____ they?

   B: Oh, _____ my classmates.

   A: _____ their names?

   B: That _____ Mieko on the left,
   and that _____ Rika on the right.

C ▷ **PAIR WORK.** Write questions for your partner. Then exchange questions. Answer your partner's questions.

> What's your father's name?

> His name is Paul.

D ▷ 🎧 **PRONUNCIATION.** Intonation. Use rising intonation in <u>yes</u> / <u>no</u> questions. Use falling intonation in information questions. Listen. Then listen again and repeat.

1. Is she French? ↗

2. Who's that? ↘

3. Are they married? ↗

4. Where are they from? ↘

CONVERSATION
PAIR WORK

Offer to introduce your partner to other classmates. Use the guide, or create a new conversation.

A: Who's that?

B: Over there? _____ name's _____.
Come. I'll introduce you.

• • •

B: _____, I'd like you to meet _____.

A: _____ …

Continue the conversation in your <u>own</u> way.

9

3 *Talk about People*

A 🎧 **VOCABULARY.** Some occupations. Listen and practice.

a computer programmer

a photographer

an interpreter

a musician

a manager

a chef

a salesperson

a flight attendant

a graphic designer

a pilot

B 🎧 **LISTENING COMPREHENSION.** Listen to the conversations about the people. Then listen again. Write the occupation and the nationality.

1. Fumiko Ito
graphic designer
Japanese

2. Lee Hyuk
_____
_____

3. Ilhan Ramic
_____
_____

4. Ana Gutierrez
_____
_____

NATIONALITIES

American
Turkish
Ecuadorian
Argentinean
Japanese
Spanish
Korean
Colombian

Partner A: Look at the top of the page.
Partner B: Look at the bottom of the page.
Ask questions and write the missing information.

Useful questions
How do you spell that?
Could you repeat that?
Could you say that louder?

PARTNER A

Name: **Paul Melin**
Occupation: **Chef**
Nationality: _____
Age: **43**
E-mail address:
_____

Name: _____
Occupation: **Photographer**
Nationality: _____
Age: **36**
E-mail address:
_____

Name: **Chisoto Nakamura**
Occupation: _____
Nationality: **Japanese**
Age: _____
E-mail address:
nakamurac@genki.com.jp

Name: **Georges Hayek**
Occupation: _____
Nationality: **Lebanese**
Age: _____
E-mail address:
hayek1435@lebworld.com

PARTNER B

Name: _____
Occupation: **Interpreter**
Nationality: _____
Age: **57**
E-mail address:

Name: **Chisoto Nakamura**
Occupation: **Musician**
Nationality: _____
Age: **24**
E-mail address:

Name: **Helena Da Silva**
Occupation: _____
Nationality: **Brazilian**
Age: _____
E-mail address:
dasilva.helena@brasnet.com

Name: **Paul Melin**
Occupation: _____
Nationality: **Canadian**
Age: _____
E-mail address:
pmelin78@interlink.com

Useful questions
How do you spell that?
Could you repeat that?
Could you say that louder?

4 ▸ *Interview a Classmate*

A **READING WARM-UP.** Do you know people who travel a lot for their jobs? Where? What are their occupations?

B 🎧 **READING.** *Top Notch* interviewed people who travel for their jobs. Read about them.

CRISTINA PETRIZZI

Meet Maria Cristina Petrizzi S. Ferreira, 38, an interpreter and translator from Brazil. She works for some well-known Brazilian and international companies. Ms. Petrizzi lives in São Paulo with her husband, Roberto, and their daughter, Natalia. But her hometown is Santos, a town on the coast. "My work is great because I travel and get to know lots of people." ■

HIDETAKA KAMIMURA

This is Dr. Hidetaka Kamimura and his family. Dr. Kamimura is a manager in a pharmaceutical company. He was born in Shizuoka, in central Japan, in 1951. Today he lives in Tokyo with his wife, Yumi, and their three children. "I travel overseas for my job several times a year," he says. "But I really like to travel with my family." ■

ARLYS DOCKENDORFF

Meet Arlys Dockendorff, 52, a photographer. Ms. Dockendorff lives near New York City, but she comes from the state of Iowa in the center of the United States. She takes photographs around the world. "I like to photograph interesting people," she says. "Musicians, artists, children, old people." You can see her photographs of Tibet on the Internet at www.echinaart.com. ■

SOURCE: authentic *Top Notch* interviews

C Read about the people again. Complete the chart. Fill in each person's occupation, age, city, and hometown.

	Occupation	Age	Lives in ...	Comes from ...
Ms. Petrizzi				
Dr. Kamimura				
Ms. Dockendorff				

TOP NOTCH
INTERACTION • *Getting to Know You*

STEP 1. **Read the articles students wrote to introduce their classmates.**

This is Kyoko Hirano. She is an international marketing manager. She is from Tokyo, Japan. Ms. Hirano is 26 years old. She lives near New York with her sister, Motoko.

Kyoko Hirano

Arturo Paz

Meet Arturo Paz. What's his occupation? Arturo is a businessman. He lives in Caracas, Venezuela. He is 40 years old and married. His wife, Margarita, is an opera singer.

STEP 2. **PAIR WORK.** **Interview a classmate. Write his or her personal information on the notepad.**

Name:	
Nickname:	
Occupation:	
Hometown:	
Age:	
Other:	

STEP 3. **WRITING.** **Write a short article about your classmate.**

Francisco is my partner. He's a bank manager. His nickname is

FREE PRACTICE

A 🎧 **LISTENING COMPREHENSION.** Listen to the conversations at an international conference. Listen again and write each person's occupation and country or hometown.

	Occupation	From . . .
1. Bill Anderson		
2. Penny Latulippe		
3. Mike Johnson		
4. Margo Brenner		

Australia
Scotland
Vancouver
the U.S.
San Diego
Peru

B Look at the pictures below. Write the occupations.

1. A _____ works in a restaurant.

2. A _____ works in an office.

3. A _____ works on an airplane.

4. A _____ works in a store.

5. A _____ works in a school.

1.　　　　　2.　　　　　3.　　　　　4.　　　　　5.

C Complete each conversation in your own way.

1. "Are you Pat?"

   YOU _____.

2. "What's your name?"

   YOU _____.

3. "Are you a new student?"

   YOU _____.

4. YOU _____?

   "I'm from Paraguay."

5. YOU _____?

   "I'm a musician."

6. YOU _____.

   "Nice to meet you, too."

D **WRITING.** Write a paragraph about yourself. Use the questions as a guide.

- What's your first and last name?
- What's your nickname?
- How old are you?
- What's your hometown?
- What's your occupation?

TOP NOTCH PROJECT
Create a class newsletter with photos to introduce your classmates.

TOP NOTCH WEBSITE
For Unit 1 online activities, visit the *Top Notch* Companion Website at www.longman.com/topnotch.

UNIT WRAP-UP

- **Vocabulary.** Look at the people and guess the occupations.
- **Social language.** Create conversations for the people.

  A: Are you _____?   A: This is _____.
  B: _____.   B: _____.

- **Grammar.** Ask and answer questions about the people.

GATE 6

MS. SMITH

XML
JAVA

✓ *Now I can...*
- ☐ get to know someone.
- ☐ offer to introduce someone.
- ☐ talk about people.
- ☐ interview a classmate.

15

Going Out

UNIT GOALS

1 Accept or decline an invitation
2 Ask for and give directions
3 Make plans to see an event
4 Talk about musical tastes

A TOPIC PREVIEW. Look at the newspaper entertainment page. Choose a concert. Circle the date of the concert on the calendar. Circle the location on the map.

THURSDAY, JUNE 19   THE GARNET CITY GAZETTE

WEEKEND LISTINGS

 LATIN

Pilar Montenegro. Latin dance-pop music from Mexico. 8 p.m. June 22. Grant Park Band Shell, Grant Park (between First and Second Ave). $25 in advance/$35 on the day of show. Tickets: 622-4408.

 CLASSICAL

Kyung-wha Chung. Korean violinist performs Debussy's Sonata for Violin and Piano. With pianist Radu Lupu. 7:15 p.m. June 20. Symphony Hall, 500 First Ave. (across from Grant Park). Tickets: $35–$75.
Box office: 622-6000.

 ROCK

Guitar Wolf. Japanese Rock Showcase. 10:30 p.m. June 21. Maxwell's, corner of Second Ave. and Market St. Tickets: $8 in advance/ $10 at the door. Box office: 622-1736.

 JAZZ

Sergio Mendes. The king of Bossa Nova jazz returns with his group, Brasil. 8:00 and 11:30 p.m. June 21. The Downbeat, 303 First Ave. Call for ticket prices: 622-1209.

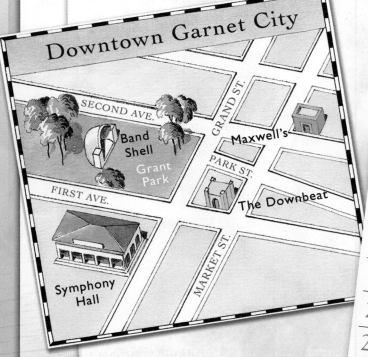

Downtown Garnet City

June

SUN	MON	TUE	WED	THU	FRI	SAT
1	2	3	4	5	6	7
8	9	10	11	12	13	14
15	16	17	18	19	20	21
22	23	24	25	26	27	28
29	30					

B PAIR WORK. Tell your partner about your choice. Where is it? When is it?

C 🎧 **SOUND BITES. Read along silently as you listen to a natural conversation.**

EVAN: Do you want to see a concert Saturday? Guitar Wolf's at Maxwell's.

MIKE: Well, thanks, but that's not for me. I'm not really a rock fan.

EVAN: What about Sergio Mendes? He's playing Saturday at the Downbeat.

MIKE: Now that's more my style!

EVAN: Great! There's a show at eleven thirty.

MIKE: Eleven thirty? That's past my bedtime!

EVAN: No problem. There's an early show at eight.

MIKE: Perfect. See you then.

D **Match the sentences with the same meaning.**

_C_ **1.** "That's past my bedtime."   **a.** I don't think I want to go to that.

_A_ **2.** "That's not for me."   **b.** I like that better.

_B_ **3.** "That's more my style."   **c.** That's too late.

E **Read the Garnet City weekend listings on page 16 again. Check ☑ true, false, or no information.**

	true	false	no information
1. Pilar Montenegro is playing at the Downbeat.		☑	
2. Sergio Mendes tickets cost $25.			☑
3. Symphony Hall is on First Avenue.	☑		
4. Guitar Wolf plays classical music.		☑	

WHAT ABOUT YOU?

Are you a music fan? What kind of music do you like? Check the boxes.

☐ Latin   ☐ Rock   ☐ Other _____

☐ Classical   ☐ Jazz

PAIR WORK. Compare your choices. Do you like the same kind of music?

Accept or Decline an Invitation

LESSON **1**

🎧 CONVERSATION **MODEL** **Read and listen.**

A: Are you free on Friday?
Married on Main Street is at
the Film Forum.
B: Really? I'd love to go. What time?
A: At seven ten.

To decline ...

B: Really? I'd love to go, but I'm
busy on Friday.
A: Too bad. Maybe some other time.

🎧 **Rhythm and intonation practice**

A **GRAMMAR.** **Prepositions of time and place**

When's the concert? What time's the movie?

Prepositions of time

on	in	at
on Saturday	in May	at 8:30
on June 7th	in 2003	at noon
on Saturday, June 5th	in the summer	at midnight
on Friday morning	in the morning	

Where's the play?

Prepositions of place

on	in	at
on Fifth Avenue	in Mexico	at the Film Forum
on the corner	in Osaka	at work
on the street	in the park	at school
	in the neighborhood	at the theater

Contractions
When's = When is
What time's = What time is
Where's = Where is

0291172

GRAMMAR BOOSTER

PAGE G3
For more ...

B **Complete the e-mail message with prepositions of time and place.**

From: val670@telcalm.net
To: hiroko_une@global.jp
Subject: African music concert

Hi Hiroko: Are you busy _on_ Monday night? There's a free concert of African music
right near your office _at_ the Stern Art Center. Sounds like a great show! It starts
_at_ 7:30. I'll be _at_ work until 5:00, but I could meet you _at_ 5:15 or 5:30 _on_
the corner of Grand and Crane. We could have something to eat before the concert. What
do you think? The price is right! —Val

C 🎧 **VOCABULARY.** Entertainment events. Listen and practice.

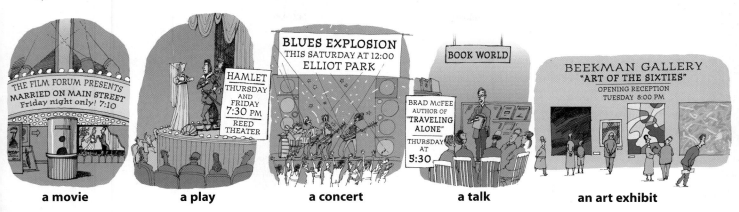

a movie   a play   a concert   a talk   an art exhibit

D **PAIR WORK.** Ask and answer questions about the events in the pictures above. Use **When**, **What time**, and **Where**.

> ❝ Where's the movie? ❞

> ❝ It's at the Film Forum. ❞

E 🎧 **LISTENING COMPREHENSION.** Listen to the conversations about entertainment events. Then listen again and complete the chart.

	Kind of event	Time of event
1.	a talk	11:30
2.		
3.		
4.		

Melbourne
WEEKEND ENTERTAINMENT

MOVIES	*Like Water for Chocolate,* Cine Metro, Sat. / Sun. 8:55
MUSIC	**The Noyz Boyz,** The Garage, Fri. Midnight
TALKS	**Novelist Toni Morrison:** "Love," Book City, Mon. 8:00
THEATER	*My Fair Lady,* Cameo Theater, Every night 8:00

CONVERSATION
PAIR WORK

Invite your partner to an event. Use these events or other events in your town.

A: Are you free _____? _____ is at _____.

B: _____ …

Continue the conversation in your own way.

Ask for and Give Directions

⌒ CONVERSATION MODEL   Read and listen.

A: Excuse me. I'm looking for The Bell Theater.

B: The Bell Theater? Do you know the address?

A: Yes. It's 101 Harper Street.

B: Oh. That's right around the corner, on the left side of the street.

A: Thanks.

If you don't know ...

B: The Bell Theater? I'm sorry, I'm not from around here.

A: Thanks, anyway.

⌒ **Rhythm and intonation practice**

A ⌒ **VOCABULARY.** Locations and directions. **Listen and practice.**

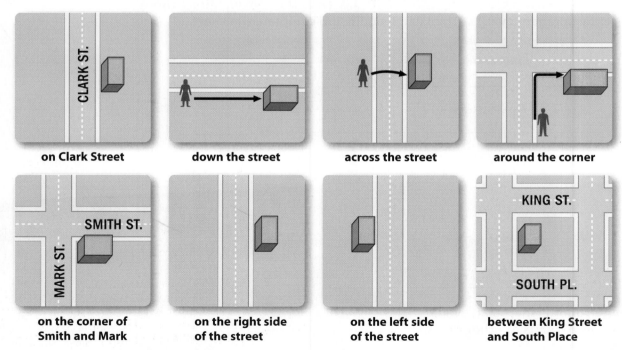

on Clark Street   down the street   across the street   around the corner

on the corner of   on the right side   on the left side   between King Street
Smith and Mark   of the street   of the street   and South Place

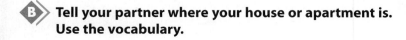

B Tell your partner where your house or apartment is. Use the vocabulary.

> " My house is on Grove Street, between Dodd Street and Park Street. "

PAIR WORK. **Practice asking about these locations and giving directions.**

- The Bell Theater
- The Film Forum
- Book World
- The Dance Palace
- Taft Symphony Hall
- Moonbucks Coffee 1
- Moonbucks Coffee 2
- The Piermont Museum of Art

Where's Book World?

It's on the corner of Holly Boulevard and Second Avenue.

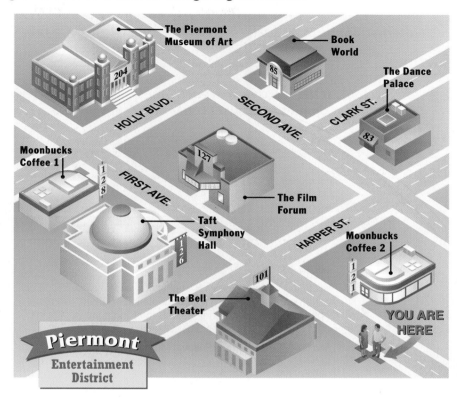

The Piermont Museum of Art

Book World

The Dance Palace

HOLLY BLVD.

SECOND AVE.

CLARK ST.

204

85

83

Moonbucks Coffee 1

FIRST AVE.

127

The Film Forum

128

Taft Symphony Hall

HARPER ST.

Moonbucks Coffee 2

126

101

121

The Bell Theater

YOU ARE HERE

Piermont
Entertainment District

🎧 **PRONUNCIATION.** **Rising intonation to confirm information.**
Repeat information with rising intonation to be sure you understand.
Listen. Then listen again and repeat.

The public library?   200 Main Street?   The mall?

CONVERSATION PAIR WORK

Ask for and give directions. Use the Piermont map or a map of <u>your</u> town or neighborhood.
Start like this:

A: Excuse me. I'm looking for _____.
B: _____? _____ …

Continue the conversation in your <u>own</u> way.

Make Plans to See an Event

A 🎧 **LISTENING COMPREHENSION.** Listen to the phone calls about events at an international arts festival. Then write either **a concert**, **a talk**, or **a play**.

1. _____ 2. _____ 3. _____

B 🎧 Now look at the March 9th event listings on the festival website. Listen to the phone calls again. Complete the event times and ticket prices.

Barrington International Arts Festival

Barrington International Arts Festival

login   update me

Saturday, March 9

Indian Ocean
INDIA

A blend of Indian classical, rock, jazz, and reggae. When traditional Indian music meets rock guitars, the result is Indian Ocean—the unique sound of India today.

when | 8:30 pm____
where | Barrington Festival Main Stage
price | US $_____

Copenhagen
NEW ZEALAND

Harborview Theater presents Michael Frayn's Tony Award–winning play. *Copenhagen* explores the impact of scientific progress on modern life.

"This tremendous new play is a piece of history, an intellectual thriller, and a psychological investigation." —*Sunday Times*, UK

when | _____ pm and _____ pm
where | Harborview Theater
price | US $_____

John Banville
IRELAND

Irish author John Banville talks about his new novel, *The Untouchable*, about British spy Anthony Blunt. "Brilliant"... "exquisitely written." —*Scotland on Sunday*, UK

when | _____
where | Ambassador Theater
price | US $_____

FIRST STREET
SECOND STREET
THIRD STREET
PRESCOTT AVENUE
AMBASSADOR AVENUE
HARBORVIEW DRIVE
Prescott Park

BARRINGTON FESTIVAL
MAP KEY
1. Main Stage
2. Harborview Theater
3. Ambassador Theater
4. Prescott Park Pavilion
🛈 Festival Information
P Parking

RPX0507 GA
G021014 C .00 ERPX0507
RPX0507 GA
*** Indian Ocean ***
MAR 9 SAT MAR 9 8:30 PM
PCOMP
1014
42877795B560
quickticket

STEP 1. **Look at some event listings for March 10.**

Barrington International Arts Festival

Latin Jam
CUBA

The Cuban ensembles Cutumba and Baobab play with local musicians for a high-energy performance of Latin music and dance. This has something for everyone.

when	10:00 pm
where	Barrington Festival Main Stage
price	US $39.00

Maori Workshop
NEW ZEALAND

Traditional works of art by Maori and other indigenous artists. During the exhibition, visitors watch the artists create traditional paintings and sculpture.

when	from 10:00 am to 5:00 pm
where	Prescott Park Pavilion
price	US $8.00 / $5.00 students

STEP 2. **PAIR WORK.** **Now make plans with a partner for the weekend of Saturday, March 9 and Sunday, March 10 at the arts festival.**

NEED HELP? **Here's language you already know:**

Invitations

Do you want to see ____ on ____?
Are you free on ____?
There's a [show] at ____.

07251968

Accept and decline

I'd love to go.
Perfect!
See you then.
I'd love to go, but I'm busy on ____.
Maybe some other time.

07251969

Ask for information

What about ____?
What time's the ____?
Where is it?

07251971

Likes and dislikes

I'm a ____ fan.
I'm not really a ____ fan.
That's past my bedtime.
That's not for me.
That's more my style.

07251972

FREE PRACTICE

Talk about Musical Tastes

A **READING WARM-UP.** Is music important in your life?

B 🎧 **READING.** *Top Notch* interviewed people about music.
Read what they said.

Music Makes the World Go 'Round!

ALFREDO LOPEZ
Mexico, sales manager

▶ I'm really into music. I listen to it all the time, especially when I travel. Mexico City is my hometown, but I live and work in Veracruz. My favorite music is pop. I prefer CDs to cassettes because the sound quality is good—better than cassettes. But most of all, I like live concerts.

KYUNG-AH SON
Korea, mother and student of English

▶ I'm a 32-year-old housewife and mother from Seoul. My daughters Han-na and Su-ji keep me very busy all day long, so I don't have much time to listen to music. I listen when they go to sleep. I like dance music, but I don't have much time to dance!

SANDRA PIKE
Canada, managing editor

▶ I'm from St. Johns, Newfoundland, but I live in New York right now. I'm a big rock fan. I also love choral music and R&B, but I always come back to rock. At work, I listen to music, quietly, if the work isn't too complicated. I recently went to a Rolling Stones concert in New York. It was fantastic!

SOURCE: authentic *Top Notch* interviews

C Read about the people again. Check ☑ each statement <u>true</u>, <u>false</u>, or <u>no information</u>. Then explain your answers.

	true	false	no information
1. Mr. Lopez likes cassettes better than CDs.	☐	☐	☐
2. Mrs. Son listens to music all day long.	☐	☐	☐
3. Ms. Pike doesn't like classical music.	☐	☐	☐

D **WHAT ABOUT YOU?** Who are you like—Mr. Lopez, Mrs. Son, or Ms. Pike?

> ❝ I'm like Alfredo Lopez. I'm really into music. ❞

STEP 1. Take the music survey.

TOP NOTCH — MUSIC SURVEY

Are you a music fan?
- ⭘ yes ⭘ no

What's your favorite kind of music?
- ⭘ rock ⭘ pop ⭘ jazz
- ⭘ R&B ⭘ Latin ⭘ classical
- ⭘ rap / hip-hop ⭘ other _____

When do you listen to music?
- ⭘ all the time ⭘ when I study
- ⭘ when I drive ⭘ when I work
- ⭘ other _____

Do you go to concerts?
- ⭘ yes ⭘ no

How do you listen to music?
- ⭘ cassettes ⭘ CDs ⭘ Internet
- ⭘ radio ⭘ other

How many CDs or cassettes do you own?
- ⭘ none ⭘ 1–50 ⭘ 50–100
- ⭘ 100–200 ⭘ more than 200

Your age [optional]
- ⭘ under 20 ⭘ 20–30
- ⭘ 31–40 ⭘ over 40

STEP 2. PAIR WORK. Compare surveys with your partner. Summarize your answers and your partner's answers on the notepad.

About me	About my partner
I'm a hip-hop fan.	Her favorite music is hip-hop.

STEP 3. DISCUSSION. Use your notepad to tell the class about yourself and your partner.

My partner and I are both hip-hop fans.

FREE PRACTICE

UNIT 2
CHECKPOINT

A **LISTENING COMPREHENSION.** **Listen to the conversations about events. Complete the chart.**

	Kind of event	Time of event
1.		
2.		
3.		

B **Complete each sentence with the name of the event.**

1. This _____ is the most popular of the season.

2. Whose paintings are at the _____?

3. Tonight's _____ is the Mexico City String Quartet.

4. Dr. Benson is giving a _____ on the native plants of the desert. Do you want to go?

5. I'm watching my favorite _____. It just came out on DVD!

C **Complete the answers.**

1. **2.** **3.** **4.**

1. Where's the bookstore? It's _____.

2. Where's the art exhibit? It's _____.

3. Where's the movie theater? It's _____.

4. Where's the house? It's _____.

D **WRITING.** **Write about yourself and your tastes in music.**

My name is Kazu Sato. I'm from Nagoya.
I'm a classical music fan. I love Mozart.

 TOP NOTCH SONG
"Going Out"
Lyrics on last page before Workbook.

 TOP NOTCH PROJECT
Bring in the entertainment page of your local newspaper. Choose an event. Then write a short note or e-mail message to a classmate inviting him or her to the event. Describe the location of the event.

 TOP NOTCH WEBSITE
For Unit 2 online activities, visit the *Top Notch* Companion Website at www.longman.com/topnotch.

UNIT WRAP-UP

- **Vocabulary.** Look at the ads. Then close your book and write the events you remember.

- **Grammar.** Ask and answer questions with <u>Where</u>, <u>When</u>, and <u>What time</u>.

- **Social language.** Make plans, suggestions, and invitations. Discuss your likes and dislikes.

OCTOBER 14

Bedford News

page 39

TODAY'S ENTERTAINMENT

"MAKES YOU LAUGH UNTIL YOU CRY"
—Alice Cabezon, *PERSON MAGAZINE*

DAVID CILLY IN
Past My Bedtime

BEDFORD MOVIE THEATER 1 7:00, 9:05, 11:10 **555-CINE**

LETHAL NOISE

NEWSTIME
"POWERFUL"

"May be one of the few horror movies that actually horrify"
—Vincent Frutilla

PLAZA THEATER
238-FLIX
9:30, midnight

OTHER LISTINGS

TALKS

Tina Truffle, *Food for Thought*, lecture, discussion, book signing. The Bookworm Bookstore, second floor cafe, 6:45 pm.

MUSIC

Saint Louis Symphony Orchestra, David Amado, conductor; Amy Oshiro, violin. Beethoven Violin Concerto; Symphony No. 6, "Pastoral." Powel Symphony Hall, 8:00 pm.

. . . .

Electric Mayhem, rock concert. The Cat Club, Midnight.

PLAYS

Phantom of the Opera. Metroplex, Hill Street Mall, 8:55 pm.

✔ **Now I can . . .**

- ☐ accept or decline an invitation.
- ☐ ask for and give directions.
- ☐ make plans to see an event.
- ☐ talk about musical tastes.

27

Talking about Families

UNIT GOALS

1 Describe your family
2 Ask about family members
3 Compare people
4 Talk about small families and large famili

A **TOPIC PREVIEW.** **Do you have lots of photos?**
Look at Linda's photo album.

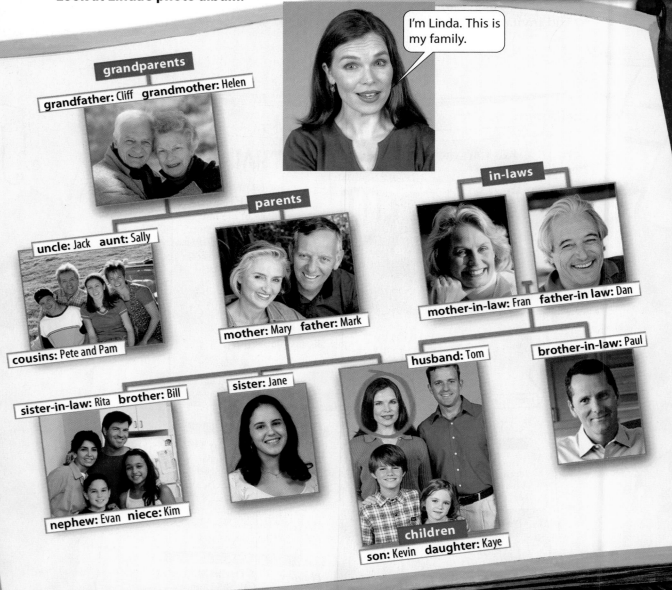

I'm Linda. This is my family.

grandparents
grandfather: Cliff   grandmother: Helen

parents

in-laws

uncle: Jack   aunt: Sally

mother: Mary   father: Mark

mother-in-law: Fran   father-in law: Dan

cousins: Pete and Pam

husband: Tom

brother-in-law: Paul

sister-in-law: Rita   brother: Bill

sister: Jane

nephew: Evan   niece: Kim

children
son: Kevin   daughter: Kaye

B 🎧 **VOCABULARY.** **Family relationships.** **Listen and practice.** 　❝Who is Pam?❞

　❝Pam is Linda's cousin.❞

C **PAIR WORK.** **Ask and answer questions about Linda's family.**
Use the vocabulary of family relationships.

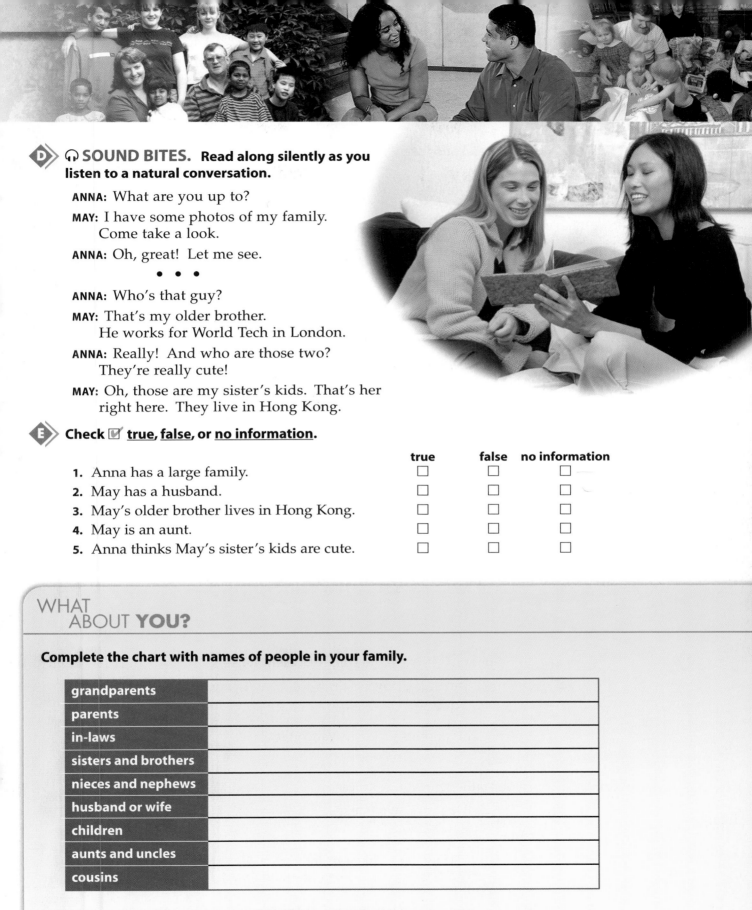

D 🎧 **SOUND BITES.** **Read along silently as you listen to a natural conversation.**

ANNA: What are you up to?

MAY: I have some photos of my family. Come take a look.

ANNA: Oh, great! Let me see.

• • •

ANNA: Who's that guy?

MAY: That's my older brother. He works for World Tech in London.

ANNA: Really! And who are those two? They're really cute!

MAY: Oh, those are my sister's kids. That's her right here. They live in Hong Kong.

E **Check ☑ true, false, or no information.**

	true	false	no information
1. Anna has a large family.	☐	☐	☐
2. May has a husband.	☐	☐	☐
3. May's older brother lives in Hong Kong.	☐	☐	☐
4. May is an aunt.	☐	☐	☐
5. Anna thinks May's sister's kids are cute.	☐	☐	☐

WHAT ABOUT **YOU?**

Complete the chart with names of people in your family.

grandparents	
parents	
in-laws	
sisters and brothers	
nieces and nephews	
husband or wife	
children	
aunts and uncles	
cousins	

Tell the class about your family.

> ❝ My parents are Blanche and Herbert. I have two brothers, David and Paul. ❞

1 Describe Your Family

🎧 CONVERSATION MODEL Read and listen.

A: Tell me something about your family.
B: Sure. What do you want to know?
A: Well, do you have any brothers or sisters?
B: I have two older brothers and a younger sister.
A: Do they look like you?
B: Not really.

🎧 **Rhythm and intonation practice**

A GRAMMAR. The simple present tense

Affirmative statements

I **live** in Rio.	He **lives** in Tokyo.
We **have** two children	She **has** four sisters.
They **work** in a school.	Sam **works** in an office.

Negative statements

I **don't live** in Japan.	She **doesn't live** in Mexico.

Yes / no questions

Do you **have** any nieces and nephews?
Does he **live** near her parents?

Short answers

Yes, I do. / No, I don't.
Yes, he does. / No, he doesn't.

GRAMMAR BOOSTER

PAGE G4
For more ...

B Complete the questions and answers with the simple present tense.

1. (have) **A:** _____ your cousin _____ any children?

        B: Yes, she _____. She _____ a son and a daughter.

2. (live) **A:** _____ your grandparents _____ in Vancouver?

        B: No, they _____. They _____ in Seattle.

3. (work) **A:** _____ your father _____ in Caracas?

        B: Yes, he _____. He _____ at a bank.

4. (look) **A:** _____ your sisters _____ like you?

        B: No, they _____. They _____ like our father.

5. (like) **A:** _____ your brother _____ rock music?

        B: Yes, he _____. He _____ rock music very much.

C 🎧 **VOCABULARY. Marital status and relationships. Listen and practice.**

They're **single**.

They're **married**.

They're **divorced**.

She's **widowed**.

He's **an only child**.

They're **twins**.

D 🎧 **LISTENING COMPREHENSION. Listen to the conversations carefully. Use the vocabulary to complete the statements about the people.**

1. He's ___married___ .

2. They're _____ .

3. She's _____ .

4. She's _____ .

5. They're _____ .

6. He's _____ .

CONVERSATION
PAIR WORK

Describe your family. Use the guide, or create a new conversation.

A: Tell me something about your family.

B: _____. What do you want to know?

A: Well, do you have any _____?

B: _____ ...

Continue the conversation in your own way.

> **To continue:**
> How about children?
> Aunts and uncles?
> Nieces and nephews?

2 Ask about Family Members

🎧 CONVERSATION MODEL Read and listen.

A: So what does your sister do?

B: She's a graphic designer. She works at Panorama Designs.

A: That's great! How about your brother?

B: He doesn't have a job right now. He's a student.

🎧 **Rhythm and intonation practice**

A GRAMMAR. The simple present tense: information questions

What does your younger brother **do**?	He works in a bank.
What do your parents **do**?	They're artists.
Where do your grandparents **live**?	They live near me.
Where does your sister **live**?	She lives in Toronto.
When do you **see** your cousins?	We visit them every summer.
How many children **do** you **have**?	I have two—a boy and a girl.
Who works at Panorama?	My sister does.

GRAMMAR BOOSTER

PAGE G5 For more …

B Complete the conversations with the simple present tense.

1. **A:** My father _____ in a restaurant.

   B: Really? _____ he do?

   A: He's a chef.

2. **A:** My brother _____ with his family in Sydney.

   B: _____ kids _____ he have?

   A: Three. I've got three nephews.

   B: That's great!

Sydney, Australia

3. **A:** _____ your sister live?

   B: She _____ in Bangkok with her family.

   A: _____ see them?

   B: I visit them every year.

Bangkok, Thailand

4. **A:** _____ your in-laws do?

   B: They both _____ at City Hospital. They're doctors.

   A: Really? Is your wife a doctor, too?

   B: No, she _____ in an office.

5. **A:** My older sister and my younger brother both _____ kids.

   B: _____ nieces and nephews _____ you _____?

   A: I have six. Four nieces and two nephews.

6. **A:** Where _____ your husband _____?

   B: He works at Harry's Shoes, on Franklin Street.

   A: Oh, I know that place! What _____ he _____ there?

   B: He's a manager.

C ▸ **PAIR WORK.** **On a separate sheet of paper, write three <u>yes</u> / <u>no</u> questions and three information questions for your partner. Write answers to your partner's questions.**

Do you have any brothers or sisters?

Yes, I do. I have three older brothers
and two younger sisters.

D ▸ 🎧 **PRONUNCIATION.** **Blending sounds. Listen and repeat the questions.**

/dʌʃi/
1. Does she have any children?

/dʌʃi/
What does she do?

/dʌzi/
2. Does he live near you?

/dʌzi/
What does he do?

CONVERSATION
PAIR WORK

Ask about your partner's family. Use the guide, or create a new conversation.

A: So what does your _____ do?

B: _____.

A: _____. How about your _____?

B: _____ …

Continue the conversation in your <u>own</u> way.

3 Compare People

A 🎧 **VOCABULARY.** Similarities and differences. **Listen and practice.**

How are you <u>alike</u>?

We **look alike**.

We wear **similar** clothes.

We **both** like basketball. She likes basketball, and I do **too**.

She doesn't like fish, and I don't **either**.

How are you <u>different</u>?

We **look different**.

We wear **different** clothes.

He likes rock music, **but** I like classical.

He likes coffee, **but** I don't.

B 🎧 **LISTENING COMPREHENSION. Listen to Frank Pascal talk about himself and his brother, Philippe. Listen for their similarities and differences. Check ☑ the statements that are true.**

Frank and Philippe . . .	
1. ☐ live in the same country	☑ live in different countries
2. ☐ look alike	☐ look different
3. ☐ have similar occupations	☐ have very different occupations
4. ☐ like the same music	☐ like different music
5. ☐ read the same things	☐ read different things
6. ☐ like the same kinds of movies	☐ like different kinds of movies

INTERACTION • *It's All in the Family*

STEP 1. On the notepad, write sentences comparing yourself to one member of your family.

> The person's name and relationship to you:
>
> How are you alike?   How are you different?

STEP 2. PAIR WORK. First tell your partner about the person you wrote about. Then discuss other people in your families.

> **❝** My brother and I are different ... **❞**

NEED HELP? **Here's language you already know:**

Ask about families

Tell me about your ____.
Do you have any ____?
How many ____ do you have?
How about ____?

How old ____?
What do / does your ____ do?
Where do / does your ____ live?

Similarities and differences

How are you alike?
How are you different?
Do you look alike?
Do you both ____?

STEP 3. WRITING. Write a paragraph comparing two people in your family.

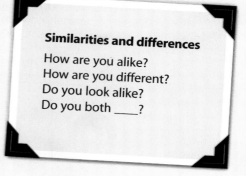

My cousin Ed and his son Ken are very different. They don't look the same. Ken is very tall, but Ed isn't. They don't like the same music. Ken likes hip-hop, and he plays music very loud. Ed likes jazz, but Ken says jazz is boring.

4 ▷ Talk about Small Families and Large Families

A **READING WARM-UP.** Do you come from a small family or a large family?

B 🎧 **READING.** Read about large and small families.

Families Come in All Sizes

On November 18, 1997, Bobbi and Kenny McCaughey of the United States were the happy parents of one child—their daughter Mikayla. The next day, they had eight children. Bobbi gave birth to septuplets—three more daughters and four new sons. At first it was very hard. They lived in a very small house and they needed lots of help. Now it is better. They live in a big house and the children help with the housework.

Barry and Julia Rollings of Canberra, Australia started with just two daughters: Alix and Briony. Then, between 1991 and 1998, they adopted six more children—five sons and one daughter. Barry also has four adult children from his first marriage. People always ask them, "How many kids do you have now?"

Julia says, "I love my family and my life!" And she adds, "Barry likes housework."

In traditional Chinese culture, families were very large. But in mainland China today, with a population of over 1,000,000,000 people, the government has a one-child policy: in most places, a family can have only one child. In the future, there will be no aunts, uncles, or cousins. Why? Because there will be no sisters or brothers.

Many people don't agree with the one-child policy. But all agree that one advantage of a small family is that parents have more money for their children.

SOURCE: www.geocities.com/juro/madhouse and www.msnbc.com

C Now read the following statements. Figure out if they are true or false, based on the information in the reading.

	true	false	no information given
1. Septuplets are seven children born at the same time.	☐	☐	☐
2. Alix and Briony Rollings are twins.	☐	☐	☐
3. Julia Rollings is Barry's first wife.	☐	☐	☐
4. The traditional Chinese family was a one-child family.	☐	☐	☐

D According to the reading, what are the advantages and disadvantages of small and large families? Match the information in the two columns.

_____ 1. an advantage of a small family

_____ 2. an advantage of a large family

_____ 3. a disadvantage of a small family

_____ 4. a disadvantage of a large family

a. Families have more money.
b. There are too many people in the house.
c. Children don't have brothers, sisters, aunts, uncles, or cousins.
d. Children help their parents with the housework.

TOP NOTCH
INTERACTION • *Small or Large?*

STEP 1. Write some more advantages and disadvantages of small and large families on the notepad.

A Small Family

Advantages	Disadvantages

A Large Family

Advantages	Disadvantages

STEP 2. DISCUSSION. What kind of family do you prefer: a small family or a large family? Tell your class why.

I prefer a small family because the parents have more time for the children.

I disagree. I think a large family is better. A family with lots of children is a happy family.

A 🎧 **LISTENING COMPREHENSION.** Listen carefully to the people talking about their families. Check ☑ if the person has a big or small family.

	big family	small family
1. Hassan	☐	☐
2. Karen	☐	☐
3. Andrew	☐	☐
4. Sandra	☐	☐

B 🎧 **Listen again.** How many children are there in each family?

1. _____ **2.** _____ **3.** _____ **4.** _____

C Complete the sentences with the correct word or words.

1. Jason doesn't have any brothers and sisters. He's an _____.

2. Harry is Henry's brother. They have the same birthdate. They are _____.

3. Nick's sister has three daughters. They are Nick's _____.

4. Gary is Teresa's husband. Gary's parents are Teresa's _____.

5. Randy's mother has a niece and a nephew. They are Randy's _____.

6. John and Carl are brothers. John's wife is Carl's _____.

7. Oliva is Ellen's mother. Alice is Ellen's daughter. Oliva is Alice's _____.

D **WRITING.** Read about Susan and Peter Wolf. Then write about them. How are they different? How are they similar?

> Susan Wolf, 28, is the manager of a clothing store in Chicago. She is short and blonde and she wears glasses. Susan is a big fan of classical music. She goes to classical concerts and has lots of classical music CDs. She likes some other kinds of music, too, but she doesn't like hip-hop or rock.
>
> Peter Wolf, 24, is Susan's younger brother. He is a rock musician and lives in Seattle. Peter has blond hair. He is tall and he wears glasses. Peter loves rock music. He doesn't like any other kind of music. He goes to rock concerts and has lots of CDs of rock musicians.

Peter is a rock music fan, but Susan likes classical music.

They both have blond hair.

TOP NOTCH PROJECT
Make a family scrapbook. Bring in photos from home. Tell your class about your family.

TOP NOTCH WEBSITE
For Unit 3 online activities, visit the *Top Notch* Companion Website at www.longman.com/topnotch.

- **Vocabulary.** Look at the Douglas family tree. Talk about the family relationships.
  Kirk Douglas is Michael Douglas's father . . .
- **Grammar.** Ask and answer questions.
  Does Michael Douglas have any brothers or sisters?
- **Writing.** Write about the Douglas family.

The Douglas Family

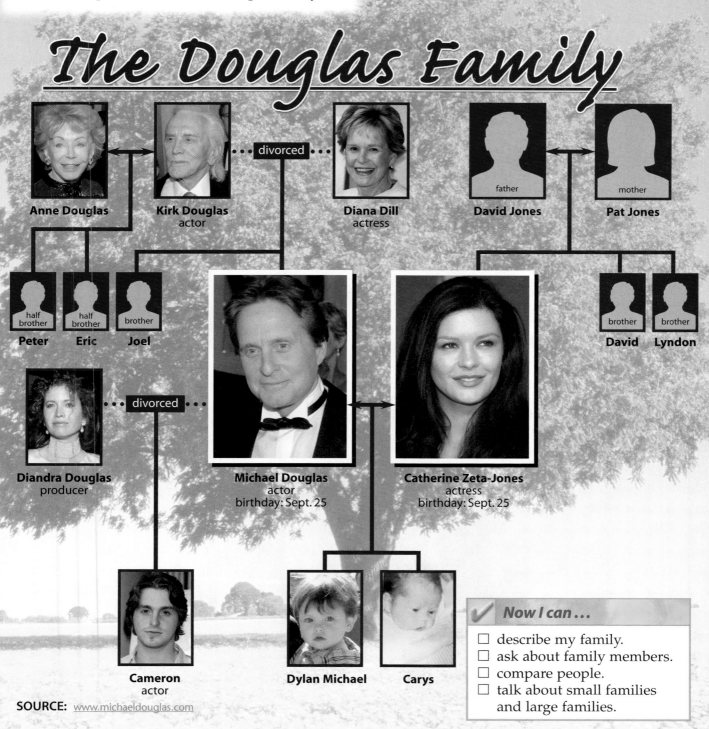

Anne Douglas

Kirk Douglas
actor

divorced

Diana Dill
actress

David Jones
father

Pat Jones
mother

half brother
Peter

half brother
Eric

brother
Joel

brother
David

brother
Lyndon

Diandra Douglas
producer

divorced

Michael Douglas
actor
birthday: Sept. 25

Catherine Zeta-Jones
actress
birthday: Sept. 25

Cameron
actor

Dylan Michael

Carys

SOURCE: www.michaeldouglas.com

Now I can . . .

- ☐ describe my family.
- ☐ ask about family members.
- ☐ compare people.
- ☐ talk about small families and large families.

Coping with Technology

A TOPIC PREVIEW. Look at the ad from a shopping catalog. Do you like catalogs that sell electronic gadgets?

THE COMMUNICATOR
Pocket electronic talking translator

- **Translates from English to eight other world languages.**
- **Displays text on screen AND correctly pronounces words and phrases.**
- **Makes world travel a breeze!**

COM445 . . . .
see page 46

B DISCUSSION. Is The Communicator a good product? Would you like to have one? Why or why not?

> **It's great for me. I like to travel.**

> **It's not a good way to learn English.**

C 🎧 **SOUND BITES.** Read along silently as you listen to a natural conversation.

CLAIRE: This printer's driving me crazy!
MARIE: What do you mean?
CLAIRE: It's not working again. It won't print.
MARIE: What's wrong with it?
CLAIRE: I don't know. It's just a lemon!

D Read the conversation carefully. Then check ☑ each statement <u>true</u>, <u>false</u>, or <u>no information</u>.

	true	false	no information
1. The printer is not printing.	☑	☐	☐
2. It's a new printer.	☐	☐	☑
3. Marie doesn't have a printer.	☐	☐	☑
4. A lemon is a good machine.	☐	☑	☐

WHAT ABOUT **YOU?**

What machines drive <u>you</u> crazy? Make a list. Use a dictionary if necessary.

my laptop

my cell phone

PAIR WORK. Compare your lists. Are they the same or different?

1 Suggest a Brand or Model

CONVERSATION MODEL Read and listen.

A: Hey, Bob! What are <u>you</u> doing here?
B: Hi, Louis. I'm looking for a laptop. Any suggestions?
A: What about a Pell? The X340 is great.
B: Really?
A: Yes. And it's inexpensive.

Rhythm and intonation practice

Positive adjectives

pretty good	☺
great	☺ ☺
terrific	☺ ☺ ☺
awesome	☺ ☺ ☺ ☺

A GRAMMAR. The present continuous

Use the present continuous for actions in progress now and for some future actions.
Form the present continuous with <u>be</u> and a present participle (base form + <u>-ing</u>).

I'**m looking** for a laptop. (action in progress now)

Tomorrow I'**m going** to Technoland. (future action)

Questions	Answers
Are you looking for a cell phone?	Yes, I am. / No, I'm not.
Is he using the computer?	Yes, he is. / No, he's not.
Are they buying the X340?	Yes, they are. / No, they're not.
What are you doing?	We're getting a new printer.
Who's buying a new cell phone?	My brother is.

GRAMMAR BOOSTER

PAGES G5–G7
For more . . .

B Read the sentences and questions. Check ☑ <u>Action in progress</u> or <u>Future action</u>.

	Action in progress	Future action
1. What are you doing this weekend?		✔
2. I'm busy right now. I'm answering my e-mails.		
3. He's leaving in thirty minutes. Hurry!		
4. Beth is at the library. She's studying for an exam.		
5. Josh isn't home right now. He's shopping for a laptop.		

VOCABULARY. **Electronics.** **Listen and practice.** **Which machines do you have? Which machines are you looking for?**

a TV	**a laptop**	**a PDA**	**a printer**	**a cell phone**	**a CD burner**

D **Complete each conversation with the present continuous.**

1. **A:** _____ to Technoland this afternoon?
   Marian / go

   B: Yes, _____ a new CD burner.
   she / buy

2. **A:** What time _____ tomorrow?
   you / leave

   B: _____ the 5:30 train.
   I / take

3. **A:** _____ for a new laptop?
   Jim / look

   B: No, _____ for a PDA.
   he / shop

4. **A:** _____ anything right now?
   you / do

   B: Yes, _____ the house.
   I / clean

E **PRONUNCIATION.** **Intonation of <u>yes</u> / <u>no</u> and information questions.**
Listen and check ☑ the boxes for rising or falling intonation.

☐ ☐ **1.** What time are you leaving?   ☐ ☐ **3.** When is she returning?

☐ ☐ **2.** Are you going today?   ☐ ☐ **4.** Is Julie buying a laptop?

CONVERSATION PAIR WORK

On sale
Super brand
Model 260

Printmore brand Great
Model GX 200

Suggest a brand or a model. Use the pictures and the guide, or create a new conversation.

A: Hey, _____! What are *you* doing here?
B: Hi, I'm looking for _____. Any suggestions?
A: What about _____? The _____ is _____.
B: Really?
A: Yes. And it's _____.

Fast!
Pell
Model 2400

DataWhiz
Model M211
Terrific!

Express Frustration about a Machine

🎧 CONVERSATION MODEL Read and listen.

A: Hello?

B: Hi, Ed. How's it going?

A: Fine, thanks. But my CD player's not working. It's driving me crazy!

B: I'm sorry to hear that. What brand is it?

A: A Tunebox. It's awful.

🎧 **Rhythm and intonation practice**

🎧 **Ways to sympathize**
I'm sorry to hear that.
That's too bad.
That's a shame.

🎧 **Negative descriptions**
pretty bad
terrible
a piece of junk
awful
a lemon

A 🎧 **VOCABULARY.** Machines at home and at work. **Listen and practice.**

a microwave oven   **a coffee maker**   **a hair dryer**   **a CD player**   **a fax machine**   **a photocopier**

B Complete each statement with the name of a machine from the vocabulary.

1. You use a _____ to make copies of documents and pictures.

2. I just got a new battery-operated _____ so I can listen to music outside.

3. I love my new _____. It can cook a chicken in minutes!

4. You use a _____ to send a copy of your document to someone else over the telephone line.

5. This _____ is making a funny sound. Maybe I'll just go out with wet hair.

C 🎧 **LISTENING COMPREHENSION.** Listen to the conversations. Write the name of each machine. Do <u>you</u> have problems with one of these machines too? Tell your partner.

Machine		Machine
1. CD player	4.	
2.	5.	
3.	6.	

Make a list of the machines and appliances in the pictures. Add machines and appliances you have in <u>your</u> house. Use a bilingual dictionary for words you don't know in English.

in the kitchen

_____

_____

_____

in the living room

_____

_____

_____

in the bedroom

_____

_____

_____

in the bathroom

_____

_____

_____

CONVERSATION
PAIR WORK

Express frustration about a machine. Use your own brands. Use the guide, or create a new conversation.

A: Hello?

B: Hi, _____. How's it going?

A: Fine, thanks. But my _____ not working. It's driving me crazy!

B: _____. What brand is it?

A: _____. It's _____.

3 Describe Features of Machines

A **READING WARM-UP.** Do you like electronic gadgets? Where do you buy them?

B 🎧 **READING.** Read and listen to the ad. Then close your book and write two sentences about the Communicator.

THE COMMUNICATOR

The pocket electronic talking translator!!

Translates to AND from English and eight other world languages. Displays text on screen and correctly pronounces words for you.

FEATURES
- It's **convenient**. Makes reading and speaking a foreign language easy and fast. Just press a button and get a translation. Save time!
- It's **popular**. Used by more travelers than any other pocket translator.
- It's **portable**. Lighter and smaller than a dictionary. Just put the Communicator in your pocket or purse and carry it anywhere.
- It's **guaranteed**. Use The Communicator for one full year. If you are not happy with our product, just return it and we will refund your money!

Battery operated. Uses 2 AAA batteries (included). Weighs just 5.5 oz. (.15 kg.)

46

C 🎧 **LISTENING COMPREHENSION.** Listen to the radio ads. Then listen again. Check the adjectives.

1

"The Sleeper"

- ☐ convenient   ☐ portable
- ☐ popular   ☐ guaranteed

2

"Cool as a Cucumber"

- ☐ convenient   ☐ portable
- ☐ popular   ☐ guaranteed

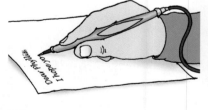

3

"The Scribbler"

- ☐ convenient   ☐ portable
- ☐ popular   ☐ guaranteed

D **PAIR WORK.** Which product would you like to have? Why?

E Complete each sentence with an adjective from the reading and listening.

1. If this hair dryer stops working, you can get your money back. It's _____.

2. This TV is _____; it's so small and light you can carry it anywhere!

3. This new cell phone is very _____. Everybody wants one.

4. I use the Coffee Pro 200 to make coffee at home. It's easy and it saves time. It's _____.

TOP NOTCH
INTERACTION • *It's the Latest Thing!*

STEP 1. **DISCUSSION.** **Read and discuss the ads. Do you like these products? Why? Why not?**

DRIVER ALARM

Avoid accidents. Alarm rings if you start to fall asleep while you are driving. Battery powered. Guaranteed to keep you awake.

SPOTLIGHT PEN

When it's too dark to see what you're writing, it's not too dark for the Spotlight Pen. The amazing Spotlight Pen lights up your paper. Won't disturb those who are sleeping nearby. Guaranteed.

STEP 2. **Write your own machines, gadgets, and appliances on the notepad.**

	Item	Brand	Description
	electric teapot	Quick-T	It's fast and convenient.
1.			
2.			
3.			

STEP 3. **GROUP WORK.** **Tell your classmates about your machines. Write your lists on the board. Discuss the products.**

NEED HELP? **Here's language you already know:**

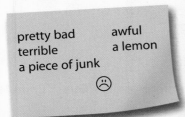

pretty bad   awful
terrible   a lemon
a piece of junk
☹

great   terrific
awesome   fast
popular   convenient
guaranteed   pretty good
☺

Complain When Things Don't Work

A 🎧 **VOCABULARY.** Ways to state a complaint. **Listen and practice.**

The window **won't open / close**.

The iron **won't turn on**.

The air-conditioning **won't turn off**.

The fridge is **making a funny sound**.

The toilet **won't flush**.

The sink **is clogged**.

B 🎧 **LISTENING COMPREHENSION.** Listen to the conversations between hotel guests and the front desk. Then listen again and write the room number for each complaint.

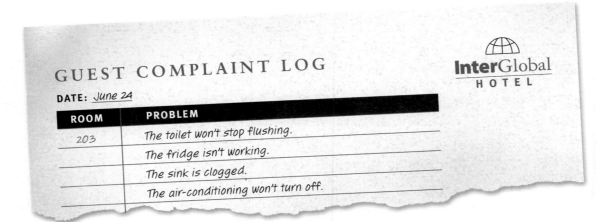

GUEST COMPLAINT LOG   InterGlobal
                                        H O T E L

DATE: _June 24_

ROOM	PROBLEM
203	The toilet won't stop flushing.
	The fridge isn't working.
	The sink is clogged.
	The air-conditioning won't turn off.

C **DISCUSSION.** Look at the vocabulary pictures and the problems on the Guest Complaint Log. Which are bad problems? Which are not so bad? Explain.

INTERACTION • *"Front Desk, Can I Help You?"*

STEP 1. Find all the problems in the hotel. Write them on the notepad.

Room or place	Problem

STEP 2. PAIR WORK. Role-play conversations between the hotel guests and the front desk clerk.

> ❝ Front desk.
> Can I help you? ❞

> ❝ This is room 211.
> Our door won't open. ❞

NEED HELP? **Here's language you already know:**

Telephone language

Hello?
This is room ___.
Can I call you back?
Bye.

State a problem

won't open / close
won't turn on / off
won't stop flushing
isn't working
is clogged
is making a funny sound
is driving me crazy

Respond

What's the problem?
I'm sorry to hear that.

A 🎧 **LISTENING COMPREHENSION.** Listen to the conversations about problems with machines. Then listen again. Write the problem.

1. _____

2. _____

3. _____

The printer is making a funny sound.

B Write a question in the present continuous.

☐ **1.** he / talk / on the phone _____?

☐ **2.** Who / use / the computer / right now _____?

☐ **3.** When / Laura / leave _____?

☐ **4.** we / go / to work tomorrow _____?

☐ **5.** When / you / buy / the tickets _____?

☐ **6.** What time / you / leave / for the concert _____?

C Check ☑ the questions in exercise B that have <u>future</u> meaning.

D Write your <u>own</u> answer to each question with real information. Use the present continuous. Use contractions.

1. Where are you going tomorrow? (YOU) _____.

2. Where are you eating dinner tonight? (YOU) _____.

3. What are you doing tomorrow? (YOU) _____.

4. What are you doing right now? (YOU) _____.

E Complete each statement with an adjective.

1. Lots of people are buying it. It's _____.

2. It's small enough to fit in your pocket. It's very _____.

3. It only takes a few seconds to do the job. It's _____.

4. It doesn't cost too much. It's very _____.

5. If it stops working, you can get your money back.
It's _____.

F **WRITING.** Write a paragraph about a machine that you own. Use your notes on page 47 for ideas.

TOP NOTCH PROJECT
Write and design ads for the best products. Include pictures or photographs. Use the ads in Unit 4 as a model.

TOP NOTCH WEBSITE
For Unit 4 online activities, visit the *Top Notch* Companion Website at www.longman.com/topnotch.

- **Vocabulary.** Look at the picture. Then close your books. Write all the machines you remember.

- **Grammar.** Ask and answer questions about what the people are doing. Use the present continuous.

- **Writing.** Write about the problems in the picture.

We fix anything

Guaranteed

✓ **Now I can...**

☐ suggest a brand or model.
☐ express frustration about a machine.
☐ describe features of machines.
☐ complain when things don't work.

Eating in, Eating out

UNIT GOALS

1 Discuss what to eat
2 Make food choices
3 Order and pay for a meal
4 Discuss food and health

A **TOPIC PREVIEW.** Read the menu. Which foods do you like? Which foods do you dislike?

World Café

Chef and Owner: Ronald Gebert

"The Best Food in the World!" Max Reed, *Journal News*, April 22

Appetizers

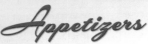

Thai grilled shrimp
Mexican black bean soup

Entrées

Brazilian steak
Fried fish Chinese style
Roast chicken

Salads

Mixed green salad
Tomato salad

Desserts

Ice cream
Apple pie
German chocolate cake

Beverages

Coffee • Tea • Soft drinks • Fruit juice
Bottled water

B Look at the menu again. Check ☑ the information you can find.

- ☑ **1.** food choices
- ☐ **2.** beverage choices
- ☐ **3.** prices
- ☐ **4.** the name of the restaurant owner
- ☐ **5.** the names of the waiters and waitresses
- ☐ **6.** the name of the chef
- ☐ **7.** a restaurant review

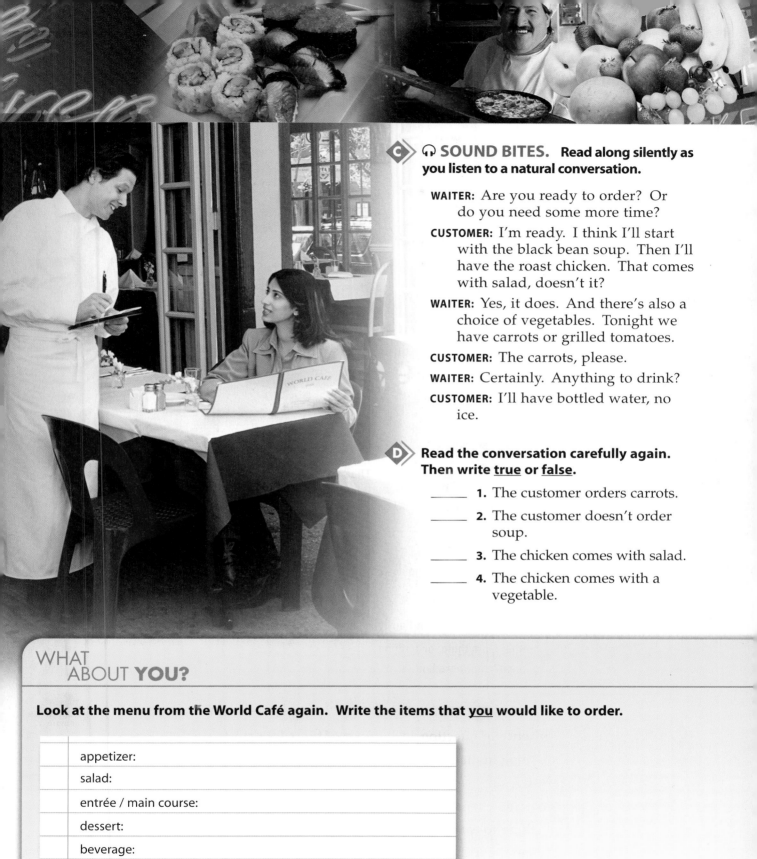

C 🎧 **SOUND BITES.** Read along silently as you listen to a natural conversation.

WAITER: Are you ready to order? Or do you need some more time?

CUSTOMER: I'm ready. I think I'll start with the black bean soup. Then I'll have the roast chicken. That comes with salad, doesn't it?

WAITER: Yes, it does. And there's also a choice of vegetables. Tonight we have carrots or grilled tomatoes.

CUSTOMER: The carrots, please.

WAITER: Certainly. Anything to drink?

CUSTOMER: I'll have bottled water, no ice.

D Read the conversation carefully again. Then write <u>true</u> or <u>false</u>.

_____ **1.** The customer orders carrots.

_____ **2.** The customer doesn't order soup.

_____ **3.** The chicken comes with salad.

_____ **4.** The chicken comes with a vegetable.

WHAT ABOUT **YOU?**

Look at the menu from the World Café again. Write the items that <u>you</u> would like to order.

appetizer:	
salad:	
entrée / main course:	
dessert:	
beverage:	

PAIR WORK. Compare your choices. Are they the same or different?

Discuss What to Eat

🎧 CONVERSATION
MODEL Read and listen.

A: What is there to eat?
B: Not much. Cheese, bread, ... eggs.
A: Is that all? I'm in the mood for seafood.
B: Sorry. You're out of luck. Let's go out!
A: Good idea!

🎧 **Rhythm and intonation practice**

A **GRAMMAR.** Count and non-count nouns / <u>there is</u> and <u>there are</u>

Count and non-count nouns

Count nouns name things you can count. They are singular or plural.

singular count noun   plural count noun
an **egg**   ten **eggs**

Non-count nouns name things you can not count. They are not singular or plural. Don't use <u>a</u>, <u>an</u>, or a number with non-count nouns.

rice   NOT <s>a rice</s>   NOT <s>rices</s>

count nouns
an appetizer   an onion
an apple   an orange
a cookie   a sandwich
an egg   a vegetable

<u>There is</u> and <u>there are</u>

Use <u>there is</u> with non-count nouns and singular count nouns.
Use <u>there are</u> with plural count nouns.

There's milk and an apple in the fridge.

There are oranges, too. But **there aren't** any vegetables.

Use <u>there is</u> with <u>something</u>, <u>anything</u>, or <u>nothing</u>.

Is there anything to eat? No, **there isn't** anything.

non-count nouns
bread   juice   rice
candy   lettuce   salt
cheese   meat   seafood
chocolate   milk   soup
coffee   pasta   sugar
fruit

GRAMMAR BOOSTER

PAGES G7–G9
For more . . .

B **Complete each sentence or question with a form of <u>there is</u> or <u>there are</u>.**

1. _Is there_ anything in the fridge?

2. _____ any cookies?

3. I hope _____ no chocolate in this cake. I'm allergic.

4. _____ anything to eat in this house? I'm hungry.

5. _____ eggs in the fridge. We could make an omelette.

6. I don't think _____ any vegetables on the menu.

7. _____ too much sugar in this coffee.

8. _____ enough lettuce to make a salad?

VOCABULARY BUILDING. Categories of food. **Add another food you know to each list. Then listen and practice.**

fruit

① apples ② bananas
③ grapes ④ oranges

_mangoes_____

_____

vegetables

⑤ carrots ⑥ peppers
⑦ broccoli ⑧ onions

_____

meat

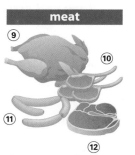

⑨ chicken ⑩ lamb
⑪ sausage ⑫ beef

_____

seafood

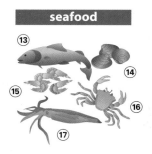

⑬ fish ⑭ clams
⑮ shrimp ⑯ crab
⑰ squid

_____

grains

⑱ pasta ⑲ rice
⑳ noodles ㉑ bread

_____

dairy products

㉒ butter ㉓ cheese
㉔ milk ㉕ yogurt

_____

oils

㉖ corn oil ㉗ olive oil
㉘ coconut oil

_____

sweets

㉙ candy ㉚ pie
㉛ cake ㉜ cookies

_____

◀D▶ **LISTENING COMPREHENSION. Listen to the conversations. Then listen again. Classify the foods in each conversation.**

1. _dairy products_____   2. _____   3. _____

4. _____   5. _____   6. _____

CONVERSATION
PAIR WORK

Discuss what to eat. Use foods <u>you</u> like and eat. Use the guide, or create a new conversation.

A: What is there to eat?
B: _____.
A: Is that all? I'm in the mood for _____.
B: _____ ...

Continue the conversation in your <u>own</u> way.

Make Food Choices

🎧 **CONVERSATION MODEL** **Read and listen.**

A: I'll have the pasta for my main course, please. What does that come with?
B: It comes with soup or a salad.
A: What kind of soup is there?
B: There's tomato soup or chicken soup.
A: I think I'll have the salad.
B: Certainly. And to drink?
A: Water, please.

🎧 **Rhythm and intonation practice**

A ▸ **GRAMMAR.** **A / an / the**

a / an
> It comes with **a salad** and **an appetizer**.

---

the

Use the to name something a second time.
> A: It comes with a salad.
> B: OK. I'll have **the salad**.

Also use the to talk about something specific.
> A: Would you like **an appetizer**? [not specific]
> B: Yes. **The fried clams** sound delicious. [specific: they're on the menu]

GRAMMAR BOOSTER

PAGES G9–G10
For more . . .

B ▸ 🎧 **PRONUNCIATION.** **The.** **Compare the pronunciation of the before consonant and vowel sounds. Read and listen. Then repeat.**

/ə/(before consonant sounds)	/i/(before vowel sounds)
the chicken	**the** orange juice
the soup	**the** onion soup
the juice	**the** apple juice
the hot appetizer	**the** appetizer
the fried eggs	**the** eggs

C **Write a, an, or the.**

HUSBAND: What do you feel like eating tonight?

WIFE: Well, _____ seafood special sounds delicious. I think I'll order that. What about you?

HUSBAND: I'm not sure. I'm really in the mood for _____ spicy dish.

WIFE: Well, what about _____ Thai chicken? Thai food is usually spicy.

HUSBAND: Sounds good.

HUSBAND: Excuse me! We're ready to order.

WAITER: Certainly. Would you like to start with _____ appetizer or soup? Our soup of the day is tortilla soup—that's _____ Mexican specialty.

HUSBAND: Is _____ tortilla soup spicy?

WAITER: Not very. But we can give you hot pepper sauce to put into it if you'd like.

HUSBAND: OK. I'll have _____ tortilla soup—with the hot sauce on the side.

WIFE: I'll have the same thing, please.

WAITER: And for your main course? We have _____ nice seafood special on _____ menu tonight.

WIFE: Good. I'll have _____ seafood special.

HUSBAND: Hmm. I love Thai food. I'll have _____ Thai chicken.

WAITER: You won't need hot sauce with that, sir!

CONVERSATION
PAIR WORK

**Make food choices from the menu with a partner.
Use the guide, or create a new conversation.**

A: I'll have the _____ for my main course, please. What does that come with?

B: _____.

A: What kind of _____ there?

B: _____.

A: I think I'll have the _____.

B: _____. And to drink?

A: _____, please.

Tonight's Specials

Soup tomato soup
         beef noodle soup

Appetizers
         seafood salad
         grilled vegetables

Main Courses all come with soup
                     or an appetizer
         grilled chicken
         pasta with clam sauce
         roast lamb

Beverages
         fruit juices   coffee
         bottled water   tea

CONTROLLED PRACTICE

Order and Pay for a Meal

A 🎧 **VOCABULARY.** What to say to a waiter or waitress. **Listen and practice.**

Excuse me!

We're ready to order.

We'll take the check, please.

Is the tip included?

Do you accept credit cards?

B 🎧 **LISTENING COMPREHENSION.** Listen to the conversations in a restaurant. Then listen again and predict the next thing the customer will say to the waiter or waitress.

1. ☐ Is the tip included in the check?   ☐ We'll take the check, please.
2. ☐ Is the tip included?   ☐ We're ready to order.
3. ☐ Excuse me!   ☐ No, thanks. We'll take the check, please.
4. ☐ Is the tip included?   ☐ Do you accept credit cards?
5. ☐ I'll have the seafood soup, please.   ☐ Excuse me!

C **PAIR WORK.** Imagine you're in a restaurant. Practice asking and answering the questions. Write the answers. Then reverse roles and do it again.

Your questions   **Your partner's answers**

1. What do you feel like eating for an appetizer?   _____

2. What do you want for a main course?   _____

3. What would you like for a beverage?   _____

4. How about a dessert? What are you in the   _____
   mood for?

INTERACTION • *Let's Eat!*

ROLE PLAY. Form groups of diners and servers at tables. Practice discussing the menu and ordering and paying for food.

LAND AND SEA

All Entrées include
Bread • Pasta or Salad • Vegetable
Coffee or Tea

APPETIZERS
Fried clams • Mini vegetable pies (2) • Shrimp salad

SOUP
French onion • Beef vegetable • Spicy fish

ENTRÉES
Steak • Chicken and rice • Mixed grilled seafood

Children's menu available

DESSERTS
Chocolate cake • Carrot cake

NEED HELP?   **Here's language you already know:**

Discuss food	**Serve food**	**Order food**	**Pay for food**
What do you feel like eating?	Are you ready to order?	Excuse me!	I'll / We'll take the check, please.
I'm in the mood for ____.	Do you need more time?	I'm / We're ready.	Is the tip included?
There's ____ on the menu.	That comes with ____.	I'd like to start with ____.	Do you accept credit cards?
The ____ sound(s) delicious!	Would you like ____?	I think I'll have ____.	
What about ____?	Anything to drink?	And then I'll have ____.	
	And to drink?	Does that come with ____?	
	And for your main course / dessert / beverage?	What kind of ____ is there?	

4 ▷ *Discuss Food and Health*

A ◯ **VOCABULARY.** Food and health. **Listen and practice.**

healthy (or healthful) good for your body
> Take care of your body! Choose foods that are healthy.

fatty containing a lot of fat or oil
> Some fatty foods are meat, fried foods, and cheese.

a portion the amount of a food that you eat at one time
> Eat at least five portions of fruit and vegetables every day.

a meal breakfast, lunch, or dinner
> Many people eat three meals a day.

a snack food you eat between meals
> Raw vegetables are a healthy low-calorie snack, but
> many people prefer high-fat snacks like potato chips and nuts.

in moderation not too much
> Eat sweets in moderation. Small portions are better.

"Veggies"

B **READING WARM-UP.** **Is eating healthy food important to you?**

C ◯ **READING.** **Read the tips from the nutrition website. Which tip do you think is the most important?**

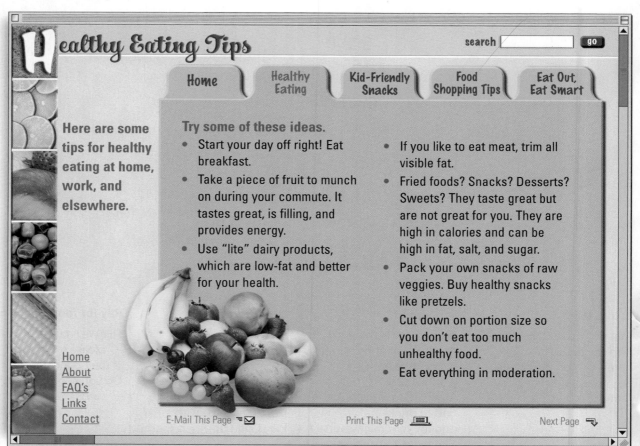

Healthy Eating Tips

search [   ] [go]

| Home | Healthy Eating | Kid-Friendly Snacks | Food Shopping Tips | Eat Out, Eat Smart |

Here are some tips for healthy eating at home, work, and elsewhere.

Try some of these ideas.

- Start your day off right! Eat breakfast.
- Take a piece of fruit to munch on during your commute. It tastes great, is filling, and provides energy.
- Use "lite" dairy products, which are low-fat and better for your health.

- If you like to eat meat, trim all visible fat.
- Fried foods? Snacks? Desserts? Sweets? They taste great but are not great for you. They are high in calories and can be high in fat, salt, and sugar.
- Pack your own snacks of raw veggies. Buy healthy snacks like pretzels.
- Cut down on portion size so you don't eat too much unhealthy food.
- Eat everything in moderation.

Home
About
FAQ's
Links
Contact

E-Mail This Page ✉   Print This Page 🖶   Next Page ⇨

SOURCE: http://www.nlm.nih.gov/medlineplus/

D UNDERSTANDING MEANING FROM CONTEXT. Use each sentence to help you understand the meaning of each underlined word or phrase.

1. Take a piece of fruit to <u>munch on</u> during your commute.
   ☐ eat   ☐ buy

2. If you like to eat meat, <u>trim</u> all visible fat.
   ☐ eat   ☐ cut off

3. Use "<u>lite</u>" dairy products which are low-fat and better for your health.
   ☐ fatty   ☐ not fatty

4. <u>Cut down on portion size</u> so you don't eat too much unhealthy food.
   ☐ Eat larger portions   ☐ Eat smaller portions

TOP NOTCH
INTERACTION • *What's Good?*

STEP 1. PAIR WORK. Together write a check mark ✔ next to the foods you think are healthy. Write an ✗ next to the foods you think are not healthy. Do you agree or disagree?

_____ rice   _____ french fries   _____ peppers and garlic   _____ ice cream

_____ nuts and chips   _____ chicken   _____ salad   _____ pasta with sauce

STEP 2. On the notepad, classify the foods from the pictures.

spicy:	*peppers and garlic*
fatty:	
salty:	
sweet:	

STEP 3. DISCUSSION. What kind of food do you like? Do you eat healthy foods? What do you eat in moderation? Discuss with your classmates.

A 🎧 **LISTENING COMPREHENSION.** Listen critically to the conversations.
Are they in a restaurant or at home? Check ☑ the boxes.

	Restaurant	Home
1.	☐	☐
2.	☐	☐
3.	☐	☐
4.	☐	☐

B Classify foods. Complete the chart with some foods in each category.

Fruit	Vegetables	Meat	Dairy products	Seafood	Grains

C Write four questions you can ask a waiter or a waitress.

1. _____?
2. _____?
3. _____?
4. _____?

D Complete with a form of <u>there is</u> or <u>there are</u>.

1. _____ too much pepper in the soup.

2. I hope _____ not too much sugar in the cake. Sugar isn't good for you.

3. I'm looking for a good restaurant. _____ any restaurants near you?

4. _____ any low-fat desserts on the menu?

5. _____ an inexpensive restaurant nearby?

6. You should eat some fruit. _____ some oranges on the kitchen table.

7. _____ enough cheese in the fridge for two sandwiches?

8. I'm in the mood for soup. What kind of soup _____ on the menu?

> 🎧 *TOP NOTCH* SONG
> "The World Café"
> Lyrics on last page before Workbook.

> *TOP NOTCH* PROJECT
> • In groups, choose traditional dishes to describe to a visitor to this country.
> • Practice describing the dishes and their ingredients, and how they taste.

> *TOP NOTCH* WEBSITE
> For Unit 5 online activities, visit the *Top Notch* Companion Website at www.longman.com/topnotch.

E **WRITING.** On a separate piece of paper, write information about food in this country for the readers of a travel newsletter.

- **Vocabulary.** Look at the pictures. Then close your book and write the names of all the foods you remember.

- **Grammar.** Write statements with <u>there is</u>/<u>there are</u> for the foods.

- **Social language.** Create conversations for the people.

- **Writing.** Write a story about the family.

LATER

✔ Now I can ...

☐ discuss what to eat.
☐ make food choices.
☐ order and pay for a meal.
☐ discuss food and health.

This is an alphabetical list of all productive vocabulary in the **Top Notch 1** units. The numbers refer to the page on which the word first appears or is defined. When a word has two meanings, both are in the list. Entries for 1A are in black. Entries for 1B are in blue.

A

a/an 56
absolutely 80
accept 58
accessory 76
accident 108
across the street 20
activity 88
actress 5
address 20
aerobics 64
agent 106
air-conditioning 48
airline 105
airplane 109
airport 66
aisle seat 102
alike 34
almost always 68
always 68
amazing 89
an 56
another 79
appetizer 52
apple 55
appliance 45
appropriate 84
around the corner 20
arrival 102
arrive 100
art exhibit 19
artist 6
at 18
athlete 6
athletic field 69
ATM 112
aunt 28
avoid 70
awesome 42
awful 44

B

back 82
bad 78
bag 76
baggage porter 118
banana 55
bank 113
bargain 116
baseball game 93
basement 82
basketball 64

basketball player 5
bathrobe 76
bathroom 45
be 90
beach 89
beautiful 78
bedroom 45
bedtime 17
beef 55
belt 76
better 78
between 20
beverage 52
big 78
bike riding 64
black 79
blazer 80
blond 38
blue 81
boarding pass 105
book 104
boring 91
both 34
bottled water 53
boxers 76
brand 42
bread 55
briefs 79
broccoli 55
brother 28
brother-in-law 28
brown 78
bullet train 101
bumpy 90
bus 109
business 4
busy 18
but 34
butter 55
buy 77

C

cake 55
call 93
camcorder 115
can 66
cancel 96
cancellation 106
candy 55
cardigan 80
carrot 55
cash 80
casual 83
CD burner 43
CD player 44

cell phone 43
certainly 80
change money 112
charge 80
cheap 78
check 58
cheese 55
chef 10
chicken 55
child 28
choice 53
clam 55
class 6
classical music 16
classmates 8
clean 64
clerk 77
clogged 48
close 48
clothes 76
clothing 79
coat 82
coconut oil 55
coffee 54
coffee maker 44
coffee shop 82
color 79
come 8
comfortable 91
complain 48
complaint 48
computer programmer 10
concert 19
conservative 85
convenient 46
cook 64
cookie 55
corn oil 55
corner 20
couch potato 65
could 103
cousin 28
crab 55
crazy 41
credit card 58
crew neck 80
cruise 90
culture 84
cute 29

D

dairy product 55
dancing 64
dark 86

daughter 5
decline 18
delay 106
delayed 100
delicious 57
depart 100
department 76
department store 76
departure 102
dessert 53
destination 109
different 34
difficult 114
digital camera 115
dinner 64
direct flight 102
directions 20
dish 57
divorced 31
do aerobics 64
down the street 20
dress 78
dress code 85
drink 92
DVD player 115

E

early 17
easy 114
eat 54
egg 54
either 34
electronic product 115
electronics 43
elevator 82
e-mail address 11
English 64
enough 116
entertainment 19
entrée 52
escalator 82
evening 68
event 19
every day 65
every weekend 65
exciting 94
expensive 78
express 102

F

fair 116
family 28

family member 31
family name 4
fan 17
fast 116
father 28
father-in-law 28
fatty 60
favorite 24
fax machine 44
ferry 109
fine 78
first 82
first name 4
fish 55
flats 80
flight 90
flight attendant 10
flight number 105
flush 48
fly 92
food 55
free 18
fridge 48
fried 56
from 6
front 82
fruit 55
funny sound 48

G

gadget 40
gate 105
get 92
get bumped 108
get seasick 108
get to know 4
get up 72
gift 77
gift wrap 77
given name 4
glasses 38
gloves 79
go 18
go down 82
go out (to eat) 54
go up 82
golf 64
golf course 69
good 78
good time 92
gorgeous 113
grains 55
grandfather 28
grandmother 28

grandparent 28
grape 55
graphic designer 10
great 42
green 81
grilled 53
ground floor 82
guaranteed 46
guitar 64
guy 29
gym 68

H

hair dryer 44
hardly ever 68
have 30
have to 66
he 8
health 60
healthful 60
healthy 60
heavy 78
helicopter 109
hello 44
her (possessive adjective) 8
hers (possessive pronoun) 80
Hi 44
him 80
hip-hop music 25
his 8
history 88
hometown 12
hosiery 76
hot 78
hot sauce 57
hotel maid 118
hotel reservation 104
house 64
housework 36
how many 32
how much 116
how often 68
how old 8
hurry 101
husband 28

I

I 8
ice 53
important 77
in 18
in moderation 60
in shape 70

in the evening 68
inappropriate 84
incredible 89
inexpensive 42
in-law 28
interesting 94
interpreter 10
introduce 5
invitation 18
iron 48
it 8
its 8

J

jacket 78
jazz 16
jeans 80
juice 54
junk food 70

K

kids 29
kitchen 45

L

lamb 55
language 4
laptop 43
large 78
last name 4
Latin music 16
leather 76
leave 92
left 20
length 78
less 78
lettuce 54
liberal 84
lift weights 64
light 78
like 30
limousine 104
lingerie 76
live 30
living room 45
loafers 80
local 102
location 20
long 78
look 30
loose 78

M

machine 41
main course 53
make (a bus or
    train) 102
manager 10
married 4
me 80
meal 60
means 109
meat 55
mechanical
    problems 108
medium 77
meet 8

memory 109
men 4
menu 52
microwave oven
    44
milk 55
miss 108
Miss 4
model 42
modest 84
more 78
morning 68
mother 28
mother-in-law 28
movie 19
MP3 player 115
Mr. 4
Mrs. 4
Ms. 4
much 54
museum 21
musician 10
my 8

N

nationality 4
nature 88
need 68
nephew 28
never 65
nice 114
nickname 8
niece 28
nightgown 76
noisy 116
non-stop flight
    102
noodles 55

O

occupation 4
office 64
often 68
oils 55
OK 89
old 81
olive oil 55
on 18
on sale 76
on time 100
on the corner 20
on the left side
    20
on the right side
    20
once a week 65
once in a while
    65
one way 102
onion 55
only child 31
open 48
orange 55
order 53
our 8

out of cash 113
out of shape 70
outerwear 76
overbooking 106
oxfords 80

P

pack 84
pair 78
pajamas 76
panties 79
pants 79
pantyhose 79
parent 28
park 69
passenger 106
pasta 55
pay 80
PDA 43
pepper 55
phone 64
photo 29
photo album 28
photocopier 44
photographer 10
physical 88
pie 55
piece of junk 44
pilot 10
play n 19
play v 64
polo shirt 80
pool 69
pop music 24
popular 46
portable 46
portion 60
pretty adj 78
pretty adv 42
price 77
price range 114
printer 41
problem 48
pumps 80
purse 83

R

R&B music 25
rain 93
rap music 25
read 64
recommendation
    115
red 77
regularly 70
relationship 28
relaxing 94
religious
    institution 85
rent a car 104
rental car 104
reserve 105
restaurant 83
rice 55
right 20

rock 16
room 49
round-trip 102
rug 116
running 64
running shoes 76

S

salad 52
sale 76
salesperson 10
salt 54
salty 61
sandals 80
sandwich 54
sausage 55
save 120
scanner 115
scary 91
scenic 91
schedule 102
seafood 55
second 82
security 106
selection 77
service 77
she 8
shopper 77
shopping 64
short 38
shorts 76
should 103
shower 64
shrimp 55
side 20
sightseeing 89
similar 34
singer 5
single 4
sink 48
sister 28
sister-in-law 28
size 77
skirt 84
skydiving 69
sleep 64
sleepwear 76
sleeves 84
small 78
snack 60
soccer 64
socks 76
sometime 66
sound 116
soup 52
souvenir 121
speak 4
special 76
spell 3
spend 92
spicy 57
squid 55
stairs 82
stapler 3

steal 96
stop 93
store directory 83
straight 82
strict 84
student 5
study 4
stuff 113
style 17
suggestion 42
superlative 114
sweater 77
sweatpants 80
sweatshirt 80
sweet 61
sweet tooth 70
sweets 55
swimming 64

T

take 82
take a shower 64
take a taxi 104
talk 19
tall 38
taxi 104
taxi driver 118
teacher 5
tennis 64
tennis court 69
terrible 44
terrific 42
than 78
the 56
theater 20
their 8
them 80
there are 54
there is 54
they 8
third 82
ticket 102
tights 76
time 18
tip n 58
tip v 112
title 4
today 68
toilet 48
tomato 52
tonight 68
too 34
top floor 82
track (athletic)
    69
track (train) 101
traffic 90
train 109
transportation
    109
travel 4
travel agency 83
traveler's check
    112

trip 89
try on 77
T-shirt 80
turn 82
turn off 48
turn on 48
turtleneck 80
TV 43
twins 31

U

uncle 28
underwear 76
unfriendly 96
unisex 76
unusual 94
us 8
usually 68

V

vacation 94
vegetable 55
visit 92
V-neck 80

W

wait 93
waiter 118
waitress 118
walking 64
want 68
warm 78
was 90
watch 64
water 56
waterproof 78
we 8
weather 89
weekend 65
weights 64
were 90
what 8
what time 32
when 68
where 8
who 8
widowed 31
wife 5
wild 121
wildlife 88
windbreaker 76
window 48
window seat 102
women 4
work n 65
work v 30
worse 78
wrong 41

Y

yogurt 55
you 8
your 8

Z

zoo 93

Social language list for 1A and 1B

This is a unit-by-unit list of all the productive social language from *Top Notch 1*.

Welcome to *Top Notch!*

Hi, my name's [Peter].
I'm [Alexandra].
Everyone calls me [Alex].
Good morning. / Good afternoon.
Good evening. / Good night.
What do you do?
I'm a [student]. And you?

[Alex], this is [Emily]. [Emily], this is [Alex].
Nice to meet you, [Emily].
Well, it was nice meeting you.
See you later.
Bye. / Good-bye.
Take it easy. / Take care.
What's this called in English?

That's right.
How do you say [your last name]?
What's your [last name], please?
I'm sorry. Could you repeat that?
Sure.
How do you spell [your first name]?
Thanks. / Thank you.

Unit 1

This is [my teacher].
Please call me [Tom].
Let me introduce you to [my wife, Carol].
Good to meet you.
Pleasure to meet you.
Are you [Bill]?

No, I'm [David].
That's [Bill] over there.
Are you [a student]?
As a matter of fact, [I am].
Is she from [São Paulo]?
Those are the [new students].
Who's that?

Come. I'll introduce you.
I'd like you to meet [Kate].
What's your name?
Where's he from?
How old are they?
Could you say that louder?

Unit 2

Do you want to see [a concert] on [Saturday]?
That's not for me.
I'm not really a [rock] fan.
What about [Sergio Mendes]?
Now that's more my style!
There's a [show] at [eleven thirty].
That's past my bedtime!
No problem.

Perfect.
See you then.
Are you free on [Friday]?
Really? (to show enthusiasm)
I'd love to go.
I'd love to go, but I'm busy on [Friday].
What time?
Too bad.
Maybe some other time.

When's the [concert]?
What time's the [movie]?
Where's the [play]?
Excuse me. (to get someone's attention)
I'm looking for [The Bell Theater].
That's right [around the corner], on the [left] side of the street.
I'm sorry, I'm not from around here.
Thanks, anyway.

Unit 3

What are you up to?
Come take a look.
Let me see.
Who's that [guy]? / Who are [those two]?
Really! (to show surprise)
Tell me something about [your family].
Sure.
What do you want to know?

Do you have any [brothers or sisters]?
I have [one younger sister].
Do they look like you?
Not really.
So what does [your sister] do?
That's great!
How about [your brother]?
How many [children] do you have?
How are you alike?

How are you different?
Do you look alike?
We wear similar clothes.
Do you both [like basketball]?
She [likes basketball], and I do too.
She doesn't [like fish], and I don't either.
He [likes coffee], but I don't.

Unit 4

This [printer] is driving me crazy!
It's not working.
It's just a lemon!
What do you mean?
What's wrong with it?
Hey, [Bob]! (as a greeting)
What are *you* doing here? (to express surprise)

I'm looking for [a laptop].
Any suggestions?
What about [a Pell]?
Really? (to ask for clarification)
How's it going?
Fine, thanks.
I'm sorry to hear that.
That's too bad. / That's a shame.

The [window] won't open / close.
The [iron] won't turn on / off.
The [fridge] is making a funny sound.
The [toilet] won't flush.
The [toilet] won't stop flushing.
The [sink] is clogged.
Hello? (to answer the telephone)
This is room [211]. Can I help you?

Unit 5

Are you ready to order?
Do you need some more time?
I think I'll start with [the soup].
Then I'll have [the chicken].
That comes with [salad], doesn't it?

There's a choice of vegetables.
Tonight we have [carrots].
Certainly.
Anything [to drink]? / And [to drink]?
What is there to [eat]?

Is that all?
I'm in the mood for [seafood].
Sorry. You're out of luck.
Let's go out!
Good idea!

I'll have the [pasta] for my [main course].
What does that come with?
What kind of [soup] is there?
I think I'll have the [salad].
What do you feel like eating [tonight]?
The [special] sounds delicious.

What about the [chicken]?
Sounds good.
Excuse me! (to get attention in a restaurant)
We're ready to order.
Would you like to start with [an appetizer]?

And for your [main course]?
We have [a nice seafood special] on the menu.
We'll take the check, please.
Is the tip included?
Do you accept credit cards?

Unit 6

Where are you off to?
I'm on my way to [the park].
Do you want to play together sometime?
That would be great.
No way.
He's a couch potato.
Too bad.

I'm crazy about [tennis].
Why don't we [play basketball] sometime?
Great idea.
When's good for you?
Sorry, I can't. (to express regret)
I have to [meet my sister at the airport].
That sounds great.

You too?
Actually, I usually go [in the evening].
How come?
Well, have a great time.
He's in shape / out of shape.
We don't eat junk food.
[They] avoid sweets.
[I have] a sweet tooth.

Unit 7

Excuse me. (to ask for assistance in a shop)
How much is that [V-neck] / are those [pants]?
That's not too bad.
Do you have it / them in [a larger size]?
It is / These are too [short].
Here you go.
Would you like to try it / them on?
No, thanks.

Would you be nice enough to [gift wrap it / them for me]?
Of course.
We have a pair in [brown].
See if they are better.
Let me see if I can find you something better.
Yes, they're fine.
I'll take the [loafers].
How would you like to pay for them?

Excuse me? (to ask for clarification)
Cash or charge?
Go straight.
Turn left / right.
Go down / up the stairs.
Take the escalator / elevator / stairs.
It's on the top / first / ground floor.
It's in the basement.
It's in the front / back.

Unit 8

When did you get back?
Just [yesterday].
Tell me about your trip.
I had a [really great] time.
I'll bet the [food] was [great].
Amazing! (to express delight)
How was the [flight]?
I was [pretty bumpy], actually.

Let me help you with your [things].
Thanks a lot.
Did you just get in?
My [flight] was [a little late].
Welcome back!
OK.
What did you do [last weekend]?
Nothing special.

What about you?
It was so [relaxing].
[The weather] was terrible.
[The people] were unfriendly.
They canceled [my flight].
Someone stole [my wallet].

Unit 9

Do you speak [English]?
I'm looking for [the bullet train].
Which one?
I'm taking that, too.
You can follow me.
It leaves from [track 15].
We should hurry.
By the way, where are you from?
No kidding!

What a small world!
Can we make the [2:00 bus]?
It left / departed [five minutes] ago.
Oh, no!
What should we do?
One way or round-trip?
I'm going to need [a rental car] in [Dubai].
What date are you arriving?

What time do you get in?
Let me check.
We had an accident / mechanical problems.
We missed our [train].
We got bumped from the flight.
We got seasick.

Unit 10

I'm almost out of cash.
Let's go in here.
What about this?
It's a bit more than I want to spend.
Maybe you could get a better price.
You think so?
It can't hurt to ask.
How much can you spend?

No more than [amount].
Could I have a look?
How much do you want for [that rug]?
This one?
The other one.
I can give you [amount].
That sounds fair.
This jacket is a bargain.

I'm sorry. That's just too much for me.
Pretty good!
What a great deal!
What a rip-off!
She got a good price.
She saved a lot of money.
He paid too much.

Pronunciation table

These are the pronunciation symbols used in *Top Notch 1*.

Vowels		Consonants			
Symbol	**Key Words**	**Symbol**	**Key Words**	**Symbol**	**Key Words**
i	beat, feed	p	pack, happy	z	zip, please, goes
ɪ	bit, did	b	back, rubber	ʃ	ship, machine, station, special, discussion
eɪ	date, paid	t	tie		
ɛ	bet, bed	d	die	ʒ	measure, vision
æ	bat, bad	k	came, key, quick	h	hot, who
ɑ	box, odd, father	g	game, guest	m	men
ɔ	bought, dog	tʃ	church, nature, watch	n	sun, know, pneumonia
oʊ	boat, road	ʤ	judge, general, major	ŋ	sung, ringing
ʊ	book, good	f	fan, photograph	w	wet, white
u	boot, food, flu	v	van	l	light, long
ʌ	but, mud, mother	θ	thing, breath	r	right, wrong
ə	banana, among	ð	then, breathe	y	yes
ɚ	shirt, murder	s	sip, city, psychology		
aɪ	bite, cry, buy, eye	t̬	butter, bottle		
aʊ	about, how	t˺	button		
ɔɪ	voice, boy				
ɪr	deer				
ɛr	bare				
ɑr	bar				
ɔr	door				
ʊr	tour				

Non-count nouns

This list is an at-a-glance reference to the non-count nouns used in *Top Notch 1*.

aerobics	candy	dancing	fruit	ice	music	running	sightseeing	traffic
air-conditioning	cash	dessert	golf	juice	nature	salad	skydiving	transportation
basketball	cheese	dinner	grain	junk food	oil	salt	sleepwear	TV
beef	chicken	electronics	health	lamb	outerwear	sausage	soccer	walking
bike riding	clothing	English	history	lettuce	pasta	seafood	soup	water
bread	coffee	entertainment	hosiery	lingerie	pepper	service	squid	weather
broccoli	crab	fish	hot sauce	meat	pie	shopping	swimming	wildlife
butter	culture	food	housework	milk	rice	shrimp	tennis	yogurt
cake								

Irregular verbs

base form	simple past	past participle	base form	simple past	past participle	base form	simple past	past participle
be	was / were	been	get	got	gotten	see	saw	seen
begin	began	begun	give	gave	given	sell	sold	sold
break	broke	broken	go	went	gone	send	sent	sent
bring	brought	brought	grow	grew	grown	sing	sang	sung
build	built	built	have	had	had	sit	sat	sat
buy	bought	bought	hear	heard	heard	sleep	slept	slept
catch	caught	caught	hit	hit	hit	speak	spoke	spoken
choose	chose	chosen	hurt	hurt	hurt	spend	spent	spent
come	came	come	keep	kept	kept	stand	stood	stood
cost	cost	cost	know	knew	knew	steal	stole	stolen
cut	cut	cut	leave	left	left	swim	swam	swum
do	did	done	lose	lost	lost	take	took	taken
drink	drank	drunk	make	made	made	teach	taught	taught
drive	drove	driven	mean	meant	meant	tell	told	told
eat	ate	eaten	meet	met	met	think	thought	thought
fall	fell	fallen	pay	paid	paid	throw	threw	thrown
find	found	found	put	put	put	understand	understood	understood
fit	fit	fit	quit	quit	quit	wake up	woke up	woken up
fly	flew	flown	read	read	read	wear	wore	worn
fall	fell	fallen	ride	rode	ridden	win	won	won
feel	felt	felt	run	run	run	write	wrote	written
forget	forgot	forgotten	say	said	said			

1A

GRAMMAR BOOSTER

The *Grammar Booster* is optional. It provides more explanation and practice, as well as additional grammar concepts.

UNIT 1 Lesson 1

Verb <u>be</u> : usage

Use the verb <u>be</u> to give information about the subject of a sentence. The subject of a sentence can be a noun or a pronoun.

| noun   subject | pronoun subject |
| The **teacher** is Chinese. | **We**'re Peruvian. |

Verb <u>be</u>: forms

Affirmative statements

There are three forms of the verb <u>be</u> in the present tense: <u>am</u>, <u>are</u>, and <u>is</u>.

I **am** a student.   We **are** married.
You **are** late.   They **are** Canadian.
He ⎫
She ⎬ **is** in the room.
It ⎭

Contracted forms

In speaking and informal writing, contract <u>be</u> with subject nouns and pronouns.

| **I am** a student. | = | **I'm** a student. | **He is** in the room. | = | **He's** in the room. |
| **You are** late. | = | **You're** late. | **Peter is** a singer. | = | **Peter's** a singer. |

Negative contractions

There are two ways to contract in negative sentences.

   He's not Brazilian. OR **He isn't** Brazilian.   **They're not** teachers. OR **They aren't** teachers.

Note: There's only one kind of negative contraction for <u>I am not</u>: <u>I'm not</u>.

Verb <u>be</u>: <u>yes</u> / <u>no</u> questions; affirmative and negative short answers

It's common to answer <u>yes</u> / <u>no</u> questions with short answers (or just <u>Yes</u> or <u>No</u>). Don't use contractions with affirmative short answers.

<u>yes</u> / <u>no</u> question	affirmative	negative
Are you a salesperson?	Yes, I am. NOT ~~Yes I'm~~.	No, I'm not.
Is he Italian?	Yes, he is. NOT ~~Yes he's~~.	No, he's not / he isn't.
Are they students?	Yes, they are. NOT ~~Yes they're~~.	No, they're not / they aren't.

 Choose an answer for each question.

_____ **1.** Are they Chinese?	**a.** Yes, it is.
_____ **2.** Are you hungry?	**b.** No, I'm not.
_____ **3.** Is he a teacher?	**c.** No, she isn't.
_____ **4.** Is she Russian?	**d.** Yes, they are.
_____ **5.** Am I in your class?	**e.** Yes, he is.
_____ **6.** Is it 3:00?	**f.** Yes, you are.

B Answer the questions with short answers.

1. Is Tokyo in China?   <u>No, it isn't</u> .

2. Is Spanish easy?   _____ .

3. Are cats animals?   _____ .

4. Is Paris a country?   _____ .

5. Are you a musician?   _____ .

6. Are Korea and Japan in Asia?   _____ .

UNIT 1 Lesson 2

Information questions with be

Use <u>Who</u> to ask about people, <u>What</u> to ask about things, <u>Where</u> to ask about places, and <u>How old</u> to ask about age.

singular nouns	plural nouns
Who's your teacher?	**Who are** the new students?
What's your name?	**What are** their names?
Where is your father from?	**Where are** your classmates from?
How old is your sister?	**How old are** your children?

Possessive nouns and possessive adjectives

Possessive nouns

Add 's to a name or a noun.

Where is **Mary's** father from?   What's your **mother's** name?

Add an apostrophe (') to plural nouns that end in -s.

What are the **students'** names?

Possessive adjectives

Where's Mary's father from? → Where's **her** father from?
What's Emilio's last name? → What's **his** last name?
What's Lee and Gan's address? → What's **their** address?

A Choose an answer for each question.

_____ 1. What's your name?

_____ 2. Where is he from?

_____ 3. Where's her mother from?

_____ 4. Who are they?

_____ 5. How old are your cousins?

a. Wales, actually. He's British.

b. Kwon-su and Toshinaga.

c. Sasha's mother? San Francisco, I think.

d. Twelve and ten.

e. I'm Milos. But everyone calls me Mishka.

B Write questions with <u>What</u> and a possessive adjective.

1. **A:** <u>What's their address</u> ?

   B: Lin and Ben's? It's 2 Bay St.

2. **A:** _____ ?

   B: His phone number? It's 21-66-55.

3. **A:** _____ ?

   B: Dave's last name? It's Bourne.

4. **A:** _____ ?

   B: Sandra's nickname is Sandy.

5. **A:** _____ ?

   B: Our number? Oh, it's 555 298-0093.

6. **A:** _____ ?

   B: Ray's? His address is 456 Rue Noire.

Prepositions of time and place

Time

Use <u>on</u> with the names of days or dates.

on Thursday	on Monday morning	on New Year's Day
on the weekend	on Sundays	on a weekday

Use <u>in</u> with periods of time (but not with names of days).

in 1998	in July	in [the] spring
in the morning	in the 20th century	in the 1950s

Use <u>at</u> with specific moments in time.

at 9:00	at ten thirty-five	at 6 o'clock
at sunrise	at noon	at midnight

Place

Use <u>on</u> with the names of streets and specific physical locations.

on Main Street	on Smith Avenue	on the corner
on the street	on the right	on the left

Use <u>in</u> with the names of cities, countries, continents, and other large locations.

in the neighborhood	in the center of town	in Caracas
in Thailand	in Africa	in the ocean

Use <u>at</u> for buildings and addresses.

at the theater	at the supermarket	at the bank
at the train station	at 10 Main Street	at 365 Smith Avenue

A **Complete each sentence or question with <u>on</u>, <u>in</u>, or <u>at</u>.**

1. When's the movie? The movie is _____ Friday _____ 8:30.

2. _____ the weekend, I'm going to the concert _____ the public library.

3. Where is he? He's not here right now. He's _____ work.

4. Where's his office? It's _____ the center of town.

5. When was her mother born? She was born _____ January 1.

6. When does the movie take place? It takes place _____ the 19th century _____ Africa.

7. There is a ticket booth _____ the center of town.

8. Is the concert hall _____ Grove Street?

9. I think the theater is _____ the right side of the street.

10. Let's go to the early show. The concert is outside, and the weather gets really hot _____ the afternoon.

11. This concert occurs every second year _____ November.

12. I'll see you _____ Thursday morning in front of the theater, OK?

Look at the tickets. Ask questions with <u>When</u> or <u>What time</u>. Ask a question with <u>Where</u>. Then write an answer to each question.

1.

★ METRO ★
HILL STREET MALL
8:55PM   Friday, Oct. 17
Phantom of the Opera

questions: _____
_____

answers: _____
_____

2.

ELECTRIC MAYHEM
MIDNIGHT CONCERT
THE CAT CLUB
SAT. OCTOBER 23 $18

questions: _____
_____

answers: _____
_____

UNIT 3 Lesson 1

The simple present tense: usage

Use the simple present tense to talk about facts and habitual actions in the present.

facts
Hank **speaks** French very well.
I **work** at 43 Fork Road.

habitual actions
I **go** to bed at 10:00 p.m. every night.
She **eats** lunch at Safi's Cafe on Fridays.

The simple present tense: form

Add <u>–s</u> to the base form of the verb for third-person singular (<u>he</u>, <u>she</u>, <u>it</u>).

I **like** Japanese food.
You **study** Korean.
They **open** at 7:00.
We **work** at a restaurant.

He **likes** Mexican food.
She **studies** English.
It **opens** at 8:00.

Use <u>don't</u> (do not) and <u>doesn't</u> (does not) and the base form of the verb to make negative statements.

I **don't go** to bed before 10:00 p.m.   Hank **doesn't speak** Spanish very well.

The simple present tense: <u>yes</u> / <u>no</u> questions

Use <u>do</u> or <u>does</u> and the base form to make <u>yes</u> / <u>no</u> questions in the simple present tense.

Do you **speak** Portuguese?   **Does** she **live** near you?   (NOT ~~Does she lives near you?~~)

Write negative sentences.

1. Hank likes jazz. (His brother) *His brother doesn't like jazz* _____

2. Vic lives in Lima. (His sisters) _____ .

3. Kate works in a hospital. (Her sister) _____ .

4. My sister has a big family. (My brother) _____ .

5. My older brother speaks Japanese. (My younger brother) _____ .

6. Han's niece takes a bus to school. (His nephew) _____ .

B **Practice. Write yes / no questions.**

1. _Does your brother_ drink coffee? No, he doesn't. My brother drinks tea.

2. _____ sister? Yes, I do. I really look like my sister.

3. _____ children? No, we don't have any yet.

4. _____ in Chile? No, my in-laws live in Argentina.

5. _____ English? Yes, she does. My niece speaks it very well.

UNIT 3 Lesson 2

┌─ **The simple present tense: form of information questions** ────────────

Use do or does and the base form of the verb to ask information questions.

> **Where do** your in-laws **live**?   **What does** your sister **do**?
> **When do** you **visit** your parents?   **What time does** she **go**?

Don't use do or does with Who. Always use the third-person singular to ask information questions with Who in the simple present tense.

> **Who** lives here? My parents **do**.

Use How many with plural nouns.

> **How many** children **do** you **have**?   **How many** books **does** she **have**?
> **How many** aunts and uncles **do** you **have**?   **How many** languages **does** he **speak**?

└──

A **Complete the questions.**

1. _____ your father _____? He's a doctor.

2. _____ your grandparents _____? They live in Seoul.

3. _____ children _____? I have two boys and three girls.

4. _____ your in-laws? We visit them on Sundays.

5. _____ your brother _____? He lives across the street from me.

6. _____ speaks French? My uncle does.

7. _____ you _____? I study early in the morning at around 7:00.

8. _____ has four children? My cousins do.

9. _____ your son _____ breakfast? He eats breakfast at 8:00.

UNIT 4 Lesson 1

┌─ **The present continuous: spelling rules** ────────────

To form a present participle, add –ing to the base form of the verb.

> talk → talk**ing**

If the base form ends in a silent (unvoiced) –e, drop the –e and add –ing.

> leave → leav**ing**

└──

In verbs of one syllable, if the last three letters are a consonant-vowel-consonant*
sequence, double the last consonant and then add **–ing** to the base form.

c   v   c
s   i   t → sitting

BUT: If the verb ends in –w, –x, or –y, don't double the final consonant.

blow → **blowing**
fix → **fixing**
say → **saying**

In verbs of more than one syllable that end in a consonant-vowel-consonant sequence,
double the last consonant only if the spoken stress is on the last syllable.

permit → permitting   BUT order → ordering

*Vowels = a, e, i, o, u
Consonants = b, c, d, f, g, h, j, k, l, m, n, p, q, r, s, t, v, w, x, y, z

A **Write the present participle for the following base forms.**

1. turn	_turning_	**7.** stop	_____	**13.** sew	_____	**19.** change	_____
2. rain	_____	**8.** exit	_____	**14.** listen	_____	**20.** be	_____
3. run	_____	**9.** sit	_____	**15.** do	_____	**21.** have	_____
4. help	_____	**10.** eat	_____	**16.** write	_____	**22.** put	_____
5. open	_____	**11.** buy	_____	**17.** begin	_____	**23.** go	_____
6. close	_____	**12.** mix	_____	**18.** use	_____		

The present continuous: statements

Form the present continuous with a form of be and the present participle.

affirmative statements
I'm **studying** English.
You're **studying** French.
He's **reading** a book.
She's **reading** a newspaper.
We're **watching** TV.
They're **watching** a video.

negative statements
I'm not **studying** French.
You're not **studying** English.
He's not **reading** a newspaper.
She's not **reading** a book.
We're not **watching** a video.
They're not **watching** TV.

B **Change each affirmative statement to a negative statement. Use contractions.**

1. She's going to the supermarket. _____.

2. He's calling his wife this afternoon. _____.

3. I'm buying tickets for a rock concert tonight. _____.

4. The Roberts are feeding their kids early. _____.

5. Jack is taking the bus to the movies. _____.

C **Write answers to the questions.**

1. Are you studying English this year? _____.

2. When are you taking a vacation? _____.

3. Is it raining now? _____ .

4. Where are you eating dinner tonight? _____ .

5. Are you listening to music now? _____ .

The present continuous: questions

Yes / no questions: Place be before the subject of the sentence.

Is she watching TV?   **Are we** meeting this afternoon?
Are you driving there?   **Are they** talking on the phone?

Information questions: Use question words to ask information questions.

When are you going?   **Who**'s talking on the phone?
What are you doing right now?   **Why** are you buying that pocket translator?

D ▷ **Complete each conversation with a question in the present continuous.**

1. **A:** _____ ?
   B: No. Evan's not watching TV right now.

2. **A:** _____ ?
   B: Yes, she's working this morning.

3. **A:** _____ ?
   B: I'm calling Janet Hammond.

4. **A:** _____ ?
   B: She's coming home later tonight.

▶ *UNIT 5 Lesson 1*

Non-count nouns: categories and verb agreement

Non-count nouns are common in the following categories:

    abstract ideas: health, advice, help, luck, fun
    sports and activities: tennis, swimming, golf, basketball
    illnesses: cancer, AIDS, diabetes, dengue
    natural events: rain, snow, wind, light, darkness
    academic subjects: English, chemistry, art, mathematics
    foods: rice, milk, sugar, coffee, fat

All non-count nouns require a singular verb.

    Fat **isn't** good for you.
    Mathematics **is** my favorite subject.

A ▷ **Complete each sentence with the correct form of the verb.**

1. Coffee _____ my favorite beverage.
   _{be}

2. Rice _____ very good for you, even when you are sick.
   _{be}

3. Influenza _____ pain and fever.
   _{cause}

4. Mathematics _____ problems for many students, but not for me!
   _{create}

5. Darkness _____ some people, but I don't know why.
   _{frighten}

6. Medical advice _____ people answer questions about their health.
   _{help}

We can make many non-count nouns countable:

bread: a **slice** of bread, a **loaf** of bread, three **pieces** of bread, two **kinds** of bread

The following phrases are used with non-count nouns in order to make them countable:

liquids: a glass of, two cups of, a liter of, six gallons of, a bottle of, a can of
solids: a cup of, a piece of, three slices of, a kilo of, a spoonful of

B **Complete each statement with a countable quantity. (Note: More than one phrase of quantity may be possible.)**

liquids

1. This soup is too salty. It has _a cup of_ salt in it!

2. She must be very thirsty. This is her third _____ water.

3. My car has a big gas tank. It holds _____ gas.

solids

4. I ate _____ cheese and now I feel sick.

5. A club sandwich doesn't have two _____ bread. It has three _____ bread.

6. I like my tea sweet. Please put in _____ sugar.

Questions with How much and How many

Ask questions with **How much** for non-count nouns. Ask questions with **How many** for count nouns.

How much rice is in the soup?   Not much. Two cups.
How many eggs are in the fridge? Not many. Eight.

C **Complete each question with How much or How many.**

1. _____ bread do we need? I put two loaves in the shopping cart.

2. _____ salt did you put in the beef stew? I can't eat it.

3. _____ hot pepper do you like? This food is already very spicy!

4. _____ spoonfuls of sugar do you want in your tea? Two, please.

5. _____ oil should I put in this salad? A half cup?

6. _____ cheese is there in the kitchen? I think we need to get some more.

7. _____ slices of bread do you want? Only one, thanks.

8. _____ cups of coffee did you drink? Your hands are shaking!

Words that can be count nouns or non-count nouns

Some nouns can be used as count or non-count nouns. The word is the same, but the meaning is different.

non-count use	count use
Chicken is delicious.	I bought two **chickens**.
Let's watch **TV**.	We have three **TVs** in our house.
The sun provides **light**.	It's too bright in here. Turn off one of the **lights**.

Plural count nouns: spelling rules

Add –s to most nouns.

cup	**cups**	appetizer	**appetizers**
apple	**apples**		

If a noun ends in a consonant and –y, change the y to i and add –es.

cherry	**cherries**	berry	**berries**

Add –es to nouns that end in –ch, –o, –s, –sh, –x, or –z.

lunch	**lunches**	radish	**radishes**
tomato	**tomatoes**	box	**boxes**
glass	**glasses**		

But do not change the y when the letter before the y is a vowel.

boy	**boys**

D **Write the plural form of the following count nouns.**

1. clam _____
2. slice _____
3. cup _____
4. olive _____

5. spoonful _____
6. pear _____
7. french fry _____
8. sandwich _____

9. vegetable _____
10. potato _____

UNIT 5 Lesson 2

A **Write a or an. If the noun is a non-count noun, write X.**

1. He has _____ diabetes.
2. She would like to eat _____ pear.
3. "_____ apple a day keeps the doctor away."
4. Would you like _____ appetizer?
5. There's _____ egg on the shelf.

6. Does the restaurant serve _____ rice with the chicken?
7. We'd like _____ water, please.
8. He always gives _____ good advice.
9. Let's go to _____ concert tonight.
10. My family loves _____ music.

Some and any

Use some and any to describe an indefinite number or amount.

There are **some** apples in the fridge. (Indefinite number: we don't know how many.)
Are there **any** oranges? (Indefinite number: no specific number being asked about.)
They are bringing us **some** coffee. (Indefinite amount: we don't know how much.)
Now we have **some**. (Indefinite amount: we don't know how much.)

Use some with non-count nouns and with plural count nouns in affirmative statements.

non-count noun   plural count noun
We need **some** milk and **some** bananas. (affirmative statement)

Use any with non-count nouns and plural count nouns in negative statements.

non-count noun   plural count noun
We don't want **any** cheese, and we don't need **any** apples.
They don't have **any**.

Use any or some in questions with count and non-count nouns.

Do you need **any** cookies or butter?
Do you need **some** cookies or butter?

Change the following sentences from affirmative to negative.

1. There is some coffee in the kitchen.
   <u>There isn't any coffee in the kitchen</u>.

2. There are some beans on the table.
   _____.

3. We have some leftovers.
   _____.

4. They need some onions for the soup.
   _____.

5. She's buying some fruit at the market.
   _____.

6. The Reeds want some eggs for breakfast.
   _____.

7. I want some butter on my sandwich.
   _____.

8. There is some chicken in the fridge.
   _____.

9. They need some cheese for the pasta.
   _____.

Complete each statement with <u>some</u> or <u>any</u>.

1. I don't want _____ more coffee, thank you.
2. There isn't _____ salt in this soup.
3. We don't see _____ sandwiches on the menu.
4. They need _____ sugar for their tea.
5. The restaurant is making _____ cakes for the party.
6. It's too bad that there isn't _____ soup.
7. I don't see _____ menus on those tables.
8. There are _____ eggs for the omelet.

🎧 TOP NOTCH POP LYRICS FOR 1A AND 1B

Going Out [Unit 2]

Do you want to see a play?
What time does the play begin?
It starts at eight. Is that OK?
I'd love to go. I'll see you then.
I heard it got some good reviews.
Where's it playing? What's the show?
It's called "One Single Life to Lose."
I'll think about it. I don't know.

(CHORUS)
Everything will be all right
when you and I go out tonight.

When Thomas Soben gives his talk—
The famous chef? That's not for me!
The doors open at nine o'clock.
There's a movie we could see.
at Smith and Second Avenue.
That's my favorite neighborhood!
I can't wait to be with you.
I can't wait to have some food.

(CHORUS)

We're going to have a good time.
Don't keep me up past my bedtime.
We'll make a date.
Tonight's the night.
It starts at eight.
The price is right!
I'm a fan of rock and roll.
Classical is more my style.
I like blues and I like soul.
Bach and Mozart make me smile!
Around the corner and down the street.
That's the entrance to the park.
There's a place where we could meet.
I wouldn't go there after dark!

(CHORUS: 2 times)

The World Café [Unit 5]

Is there something that you want?
Is there anything you need?
Have you made up your mind
what you want to eat?
Place your order now,
or do you need more time?
Why not start with some juice—
lemon, orange, or lime?
Some like it hot, some like it sweet,
some like it really spicy.
You may not like everything you eat,
but I think we're doing nicely.

(CHORUS)
I can understand every word you say.
Tonight we're speaking English at The
World Café.

I'll take the main course now.
I think I'll have the fish.
Does it come with a choice of another
  dish?
Excuse me waiter, please—
I think I'm in the mood
for a little dessert, and the cake looks good.

Do you know? Are there any low-fat
desserts that we could try now?
I feel like having a bowl of fruit.
Do you have to say good-bye now?

(CHORUS)

Apples, oranges, cheese and ham,
coffee, juice, milk, bread, and jam,
rice and beans, meat and potatoes,
eggs and ice cream,
grilled tomatoes—
That's the menu.
That's the list.
Is there anything I missed?

(CHORUS)

A Typical Day [Unit 6]

The Couch Potato sits around.
He eats junk food by the pound.
It's just a typical day.
Watching as the world goes by,
he's out of shape and wonders why.
It's just a typical day.

(CHORUS)
Every night he dreams that he's
skydiving through the air.
And sometimes you appear.
He says, "What are you doing here?"

He cleans the house and plays guitar,
takes a shower, drives the car.
It's just a typical day.
He watches TV all alone,
reads and sleeps, talks on the phone.
It's just a typical day.

(CHORUS)

I'm sorry.
Mr. Couch Potato's resting right now.
Can he call you back?
He usually lies down every day of the week,
and he always has to have a snack.
Now all his dreams are coming true.
He's making plans to be with you.
It's just a typical day.
He goes dancing once a week.
He's at the theater as we speak!
It's just a typical day.

(CHORUS)

My Dream Vacation [Unit 8]

The ride was bumpy
and much too long.
It was pretty boring.
It felt so wrong.
I slept all night,
and it rained all day.
We left the road,
and we lost the way.
Then you came along
and you took my hand.
You whispered words
I could understand.

(CHORUS)
On my dream vacation,
I dream of you.

I don't ever want to wake up.
On my dream vacation,
this much is true:
I don't ever want it to stop.

The food was awful.
They stole my purse.
The whole two weeks went
from bad to worse.
They canceled my ticket.
I missed my flight.
They were so unfriendly
it just wasn't right.
So I called a taxi,
and I got inside,
and there you were,
sitting by my side.

(CHORUS)

You were so unusual.
The day was so exciting.
I opened up my eyes,
and you were gone.
I waited for hours.
You never called.
I watched TV
and looked at the walls.
Where did you go to?
Why weren't you near?
Did you have a reason
to disappear?
So I flew a plane
to the south of France,
and I heard you say,
"Would you like to dance?"

(CHORUS)

Shopping for Souvenirs [Unit 10]

I go to the bank at a quarter to ten.
I pick up my cash from the ATM.
Here at the store, it won't be too hard
to take out a check or a credit card.
The bank has a good rate of exchange,
and everything here is in my price range.
The easiest part of this bargain hunt
is that I can afford anything I want.

(CHORUS)
Whenever I travel around the world,
I spend my money for two.
Shopping for souvenirs
helps me to be near you.

I try to decide how much I should pay
for the beautiful art I see on display.
To get a great deal, I can't be too nice.
It can't hurt to ask for a better price.

(CHORUS)

Yes, it's gorgeous, and I love it.
It's the biggest and the best,
though it might not be the cheapest.
How much is it—more than all the rest?
I'll pass on some good advice to you:
When you're in Rome, do as the Romans do.
A ten percent tip for the taxi fare
should be good enough when you're staying
  there.

(CHORUS)

TOP NOTCH POP LYRICS

TOP NOTCH   1A

Workbook

Joan Saslow ■ Allen Ascher

with Barbara R. Denman

PEARSON
Longman

UNIT 1

Getting Acquainted

TOPIC PREVIEW

1 Read about the famous person. Then check ✔ <u>true</u>, <u>false</u>, or <u>no information</u> according to the website.

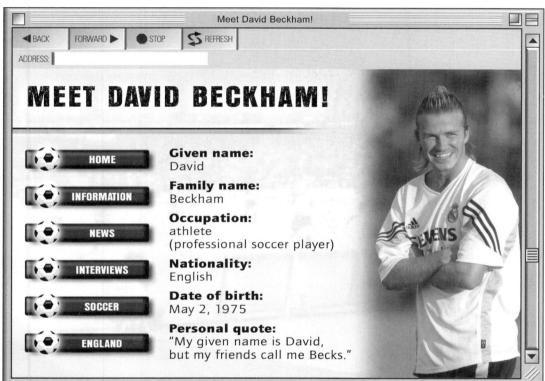

Source: www.beckham-magazine.com

	true	false	no information
1. His first name is David.	☐	☐	☐
2. His last name is Becks.	☐	☐	☐
3. He is an actor.	☐	☐	☐
4. He is married.	☐	☐	☐
5. His friends call him David.	☐	☐	☐

2 Match the word or words with the same meaning. Draw a line.

1. Nice to meet you.   **a.** not married
2. first name   **b.** given name
3. last name   **c.** Good to meet you.
4. single   **d.** family name

3 WHAT ABOUT YOU? Complete the information. Write <u>your</u> name on the lines.

> ## HELLO
>
> MY NAME IS _____.
>   first name   last name
>
> PLEASE CALL ME _____.

LESSON 1

4 Choose the correct response. Circle the letter.

1. "It's a pleasure to meet you, Choi."
   a. Good.   b. Yes, I am.   c. You, too.

2. "Are you new here?"
   a. Yes, we are.   b. Yes, they are.   c. Yes, he is.

3. "Is Mr. Adams married?"
   a. No, she isn't.   b. No, he isn't.   c. Yes, they are.

4. "Are you John?"
   a. That's Sam over there.   b. Nice to meet you, John.   c. As a matter of fact, I am.

5 Complete the conversations. Use words from the box.

meet	over	think	too	that	am	is

1. **A:** Are you a student here?

   B: Yes, I _____. I'm Tanja.

   A: I'm Claudio. It's nice to _____ you, Tanja.

   B: You, _____, Claudio.

2. **A:** Is _____ the new manager _____ there?

   B: Yes. That's Ms. Douglas. She's from New Zealand.

   A: _____ she from Wellington?

   B: No, she isn't. I _____ she's from Auckland.

6 Look at the responses. Complete the <u>yes</u> / <u>no</u> questions with <u>be</u>.

1. **A:** *Are you* Stacey?
   B: No, I'm not. I'm Claire.

2. **A:** _____ English?
   B: No, they're not. They're Australian.

3. **A:** _____ a student here?
   B: Yes, she is. She's new.

4. **A:** _____ married?
   B: No, he's not. He's single.

5. **A:** _____ in our class?
   B: Yes, we are.

6. **A:** _____ an art teacher?
   B: Yes, as a matter of fact, I am.

Look at the pictures. Write short answers about the people.

We're students.

Andy and Tara

I'm a soccer player.

John

1. Are Andy and Tara students?

Yes, they are .

2. Is John an athlete?

_____ .

I'm from Mexico.

MEXICO

MEXICO

Maria

This is my wife, Linda.

Linda and Mike

3. Is Maria from Venezuela?

_____ .

4. Are Linda and Mike married?

_____ .

8 **CHALLENGE. Write yes / no questions and give short answers.**
Use contractions when possible.

1. A: _Are you Paul_ ?

   B: _No, I'm not_ .
   (I am not Paul.)

2. A: _Are they the new teachers_ ?

   B: _Yes, they are_ .
   (They are the new teachers.)

3. A: _____ ?

   B: _____ .
   (He's not married.)

4. A: _____ ?

   B: _____ .
   (We're from Kyoto.)

5. A: _____ ?

   B: _____ .
   (Bill and Cliff aren't here today.)

6. A: _____ ?

   B: _____ .
   (She's from Ireland.)

7. A: _____ ?

   B: _____ .
   (I'm not in your class.)

9 WHAT ABOUT YOU? Answer the questions. Use your <u>own</u> words.

1. "Are you a new student?" YOU _____.

2. "Are you an athlete?" YOU _____.

3. "Are you married?" YOU _____.

LESSON 2

10 Complete the conversations. Use words from the box.

they	their	you	your	he	his	she	her	we	our

1. A: Who's that?
   B: That's Ajit's brother. _____ name is Rajeev,
   but everyone calls him Raj.
   A: How old is _____?
   B: Twenty-three, I think.

2. A: Are _____ the new English teacher?
   B: Yes, I am.
   A: Hi, I'm Steve. What's _____ name?
   B: Doug Stearns. But everyone calls me DJ.

3. A: These are my two sons.
   B: What are _____ names?
   A: Todd and Allen.
   B: Are _____ students?
   A: Yes, they are.

4. A: Hi, Ha-na.
   B: Hello, Su-ji. Are _____ classmates again?
   A: Yes, I think so. Is that _____ teacher over there?
   B: Yes. _____ name is Mrs. Kim.
   A: _____ looks very young!

Most Popular Family Names

Country	Family Name
China	Li
France	Martin
Great Britain	Smith
India	Patel
Japan	Sato
Korea	Kim
Russia	Ivanov
Spain	Garcia
United States	Smith
Vietnam	Nguyen

11 Complete the information questions. Use contractions when possible.

1. A: _Who's_____ that?
   B: That's Mr. Matz.

2. A: _____ his occupation?
   B: He's an artist.

3. A: Your daughter is very cute.
   _____ she?
   B: She's eight months old.

4. A: I'll send you an e-mail.
   _____ your e-mail address?
   B: It's une-yoshiko@videotech.co.jp.

5. A: _____ Anil and Temel from?
   B: They're from Istanbul, I think.

6. A: _____ your new classmates?
   B: That's Marcos on the right and Paulo
   on the left.

12 Choose the correct response. Write the letter on the line.

1. ____ "How old is Michael?"
2. ____ "Who's not here?"
3. ____ "What are your occupations?"
4. ____ "Where are their friends from?"
5. ____ "Where is Diana?"
6. ____ "What's that?"
7. ____ "Who are your teachers?"

a. She's over there.
b. They're from Germany.
c. He's three.
d. Rachel isn't here.
e. Their names are Mr. Park and Ms. Kim.
f. I'm a singer, and he's a student.
g. That's a student information form.

13 Look at the picture. Write a question for each answer.

1. A: _____?
   B: They're my friends from computer class.

2. A: _____?
   B: Their names are Juan and Paloma.

3. A: _____?
   B: Spain.

4. A: _____?
   B: She's two years old.

14 WHAT ABOUT YOU? Answer the questions. Use your <u>own</u> words.

1. "What's your occupation?" **YOU** _____.

2. "Who's under 15 years old in your family?" **YOU** _____.

3. "What's your mother's name?" **YOU** _____.

4. "How old are you?" **YOU** _____.

LESSONS 3 AND 4

 15 Read the letter and reply on an intercultural exchange website.

Ask Allen

Advice for International Travelers

Intercultural Exchange.com

What's in a first name? In many countries, it's the last.

Dear Allen,

I have a problem. My name is Chinese. It's Zhang Yin. Zhang is my last name and Yin is my first name. In China, family names are first and given names are last. I'm a salesman and I often travel to English-speaking countries for business. When I fill out a personal information form in English, I write <u>Yin</u> in the box for first name and <u>Zhang</u> in the box for last name. Then people call me Yin Zhang. When I introduce myself as Zhang Yin, they call me Mr. Yin. So sometimes I say that my name is Yin Zhang. But I don't feel comfortable with that because that isn't my real name. What should I do?

Zhang Yin
Shanghai, China

Dear Yin,

In English-speaking countries, when you ask, "What's your name?" you always get the person's given name first and the family name last. In China, and in many Asian countries, including Japan and Korea, the family name is first and given name is second. To avoid confusion, try introducing yourself like this: "Hi. I'm Zhang Yin. My first name is Yin and my family name is Zhang. Please call me Mr. Zhang."

Allen

Now read the sentences. Check ✔ <u>true</u>, <u>false</u>, or <u>no information</u>.

	true	false	no information
1. Zhang Yin's family name is Yin.	☐	☐	☐
2. Zhang Yin is a pilot.	☐	☐	☐
3. In China, you say a person's family name first and given name last.	☐	☐	☐
4. Zhang Yin is from China.	☐	☐	☐
5. Zhang Yin is married.	☐	☐	☐

16 **WHAT ABOUT YOU?** Answer the questions. Use your <u>own</u> words.

1. "In this country, are family names first or are given names first?"

   (YOU) _____.

2. "What's your nickname?"

   (YOU) _____.

3. "What do you call your teacher?"

   (YOU) _____.

17 **Read the questions. Who is it OK to say this to? Check ✔ <u>OK</u> or <u>Not OK</u>.**

Question	Person to ask	OK	Not OK
1. What's your first name?	your friend's friend	☐	☐
2. Are you married?	your manager	☐	☐
3. How old are you?	your teacher	☐	☐
4. What do you do?	your father's friend	☐	☐
5. What's your nickname?	your friend's grandfather	☐	☐
6. Where are you from?	your classmate	☐	☐

 18 **Read about a famous athlete.**

Name:	Eldrick Woods
Nickname:	Tiger
Occupation:	Professional Athlete (Golfer)
Date of birth:	December 30, 1975
Nationality:	American
Hometown:	Cypress, California, USA
Now lives in:	Orlando, Florida, USA
Interesting fact:	Tiger started playing golf when he was only nine months old and played golf on a TV show when he was two!

SOURCE: <u>www.tigerwoods.com</u>

Now write a short biography of Mr. Woods. Use the biographies on page 13 in the Student's Book as a model.

GRAMMAR
BOOSTER

A ▸ **Choose the correct response. Circle the letter.**

1. "Are you from Italy?"
   a. Yes, I am. **b.** No, he's not. **c.** Yes, they are.

2. "Is she late?"
   a. No, she is. **b.** Yes, we are. **c.** Yes, she is.

3. "Are they teachers?"
   a. No, I'm not. **b.** Yes, they are. **c.** No, she isn't.

4. "Is Canada a language?"
   a. Yes, she is. **b.** No, it isn't. **c.** Yes, it is.

5. "Is Jim married?"
   a. Yes, they are. **b.** Yes, he is. **c.** Yes, I am.

B ▸ **Choose the correct response. Write the letter on the line.**

1. _____ "Are you a musician?"   **a.** His name's Ivan.

2. _____ "Where are your parents from?" **b.** No, I'm a graphic designer.

3. _____ "How old are you?"   **c.** He's a manager.

4. _____ "What's her nationality?"   **d.** São Paulo. But they live in Santos now.

5. _____ "What's his occupation?"   **e.** Twenty.

6. _____ "Who's your friend?"   **f.** She's Australian.

C ▸ **Complete the conversations. Use contractions when possible.**

1. **A:** Is she Chinese?
   B: No, _she's_____ Russian.

2. **A:** Who's that?
   B: _____ my teacher. His name is Mr. Hopkins.

3. **A:** What's their last name?
   B: _____ Johnson.

4. **A:** How old is your brother?
   B: _____ twenty-three.

5. **A:** Where's London?
   B: _____ in England.

6. **A:** What are your children's names?
   B: _____ Daniel and Susana.

7. **A:** Am I late for class?
   B: No, _____ late.

8. **A:** Are you a flight attendant?
   B: No, _____ a pilot.

D Complete the sentences with a possessive adjective from the box.

| my | your | his | her | our | their |

1. Cindy and Lee are new students. _____ teacher is Mr. Michaels.

2. Mr. Vidal is a computer programmer. _____ family lives in Paris.

3. Mrs. Ichikawa is from Tokyo. _____ nationality is Japanese.

4. Are you a chef? _____ chicken is very good.

5. I have two sisters. _____ sister Sarah lives in London and _____ sister Ellen lives in Brighton.

6. Sally and I are in a computer class. _____ class is at 9 a.m.

E Look at the responses. Write information questions. Use contractions when possible.

1. **A:** _How old is your son_ _____?

   B: My son? He's sixteen.

2. **A:** _____?

   B: My teacher's name is Linda Thomas.

3. **A:** _____?

   B: I'm from Turkey.

4. **A:** _____?

   B: They're students.

5. **A:** _____?

   B: It's Margaret. But my nickname is Meg.

6. **A:** _____?

   B: My address? It's 1932 West Street.

JUST FOR **FUN**

 1 Find the words in the puzzle. Circle each word. Words can be across (→) or down (↓).

~~manager~~

salesperson

teacher

interpreter

programmer

photographer

designer

pilot

musician

chef

p	m	a	n	a	g	e	r	z	g	h	p	l
d	g	p	d	z	f	c	h	m	l	w	v	d
e	x	i	v	y	d	h	d	u	j	q	t	k
s	a	l	e	s	p	e	r	s	o	n	e	z
i	c	o	z	i	p	f	w	i	g	c	a	a
g	u	t	d	y	k	e	b	c	h	d	c	g
n	i	o	q	l	u	r	h	i	t	y	h	m
e	p	h	o	t	o	g	r	a	p	h	e	r
r	n	d	v	t	c	p	t	n	r	k	r	w
p	r	o	g	r	a	m	m	e	r	w	s	z
f	i	n	t	e	r	p	r	e	t	e	r	y

 2 Find the nationality. Unscramble the letters.

1. Maxecni = _____

2. Ciananad = _____

3. Tishruk = _____

4. Antigreenan = _____

5. Banliziar = _____

6. Lanseebe = _____

UNIT 2

Going out

TOPIC PREVIEW

1 ▷ Look at the newspaper concert listings. Then complete the chart.

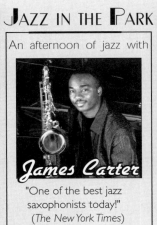

Who is playing?	What kind of music?	Where is it?	What time is the show?	How much are tickets?
Marc Anthony	Latin		10:30 p.m.	
James Carter		Riverfront Park		
				$15
	classical	City Music Hall		

2 ▷ **WHAT ABOUT YOU?** **What's your style?** Check ☑ Not for me or More my style.

Kind of concert	Not for me	More my style
an afternoon jazz concert in the park	☐	☐
a late night rock concert at a rock club	☐	☐
a Latin music concert at a dance club	☐	☐
a classical concert at a concert hall	☐	☐

What's past your bedtime?
Circle the times.
9:30 PM   10:30 PM   11:30 PM
12:30 AM   2:30 AM

3 ▸ **WHAT ABOUT YOU? Complete the paragraph with kinds of music and concert times. Use your <u>own</u> words.**

I like _____ music, but _____ music isn't really my style. A concert at _____ is too late, but a concert at _____ is perfect for me.

LESSON 1

4 ▸ **Choose the correct response. Circle the letter.**

1. "What time's the show?"
   a. At the theater.　　　**b.** On Tuesday.　　　　**c.** At 8:30.

2. "I'm busy on Saturday. What about Friday?"
   a. I'm not really a fan.　**b.** Perfect.　　　　　**c.** Too bad.

3. "Where's the concert?"
   a. Really? I'd love to go.　**b.** In the park.　　　**c.** At noon.

4. "Do you want to see an art exhibit on Sunday?"
   a. I'd love to.　　　　　**b.** That's past my bedtime.　**c.** On Monday.

5 ▸ **Put the conversation in order. Write the number on the line.**

_1_ Are you busy on Saturday night?

___ 10:00 p.m.? Well, I'd like to go, but that's past my bedtime.

___ Really? Sounds great! What time's the play?

___ *A Comedy of Errors* is at the Community Theater.

___ At 10:00 p.m. It's a late show.

___ No, I'm not. Why?

_7_ Too bad. Maybe some other time.

6 ▸ **Complete the sentences with <u>on</u>, <u>in</u>, or <u>at</u>.**

1. The movie theater is _____ Dewey Street.

2. Ana isn't here. She's _____ New York.

3. My music class is _____ the New City Music School. It's _____ the corner of Main and Park.

4. The talk is _____ 11:00 _____ the morning.

5. The play is _____ noon, _____ the park.

6. The Marc Anthony concert is _____ Friday, January 18th.

7. I can't talk right now. I'm _____ work. I'll call you when I get home.

7 ▸ **Write questions with <u>When</u>, <u>Where</u>, or <u>What time</u>. Use contractions when possible.**

1. **A:** *When's the play* _____? **B:** The play is on Wednesday.

2. **A:** _____? **B:** The concert is at 7:00.

3. **A:** _____? **B:** The school is on Newton Street.

4. **A:** _____? **B:** Tim's at work.

5. **A:** _____? **B:** His class is on Monday morning.

6. **A:** _____? **B:** The concert is in the park.

7. **A:** _____? **B:** My class is at 10:30.

8 ▷ **WHAT ABOUT YOU?** Answer the questions. Use your <u>own</u> words. Use <u>in</u>, <u>on</u>, or <u>at</u>.

1. "Where is your school?" (YOU) _____.

2. "What time is your English class?" (YOU) _____.

3. "When are you free this week?" (YOU) _____.

LESSON 2

9 ▷ **Choose the correct responses to complete the conversation. Write the letter on the line.**

A: Excuse me. I'm looking for Gino's Café.

B: _____
   1.

A: Yes. Is it around here?

B: _____
   2.

A: It's 610 Pine Street.

B: _____
   3.

A: Really? That's great. Thanks.

B: _____
   4.

a. Well, Pine Street is right around the corner.

b. I think it is. Do you know the address?

c. No problem.

d. Gino's? The Italian Café?

10 ▷ **Look at the pictures. Write the locations on the line. Use words from the box.**

around the corner   ~~on~~   down the street   across the street   on the corner of   on the left

1. *It's on Route 198* .

2. _____ .

3. _____ .

4. _____ .

5. _____ .

6. _____ .

11 CHALLENGE. **Complete the conversation. Use the map and your <u>own</u> words.**

A: Excuse me. I'm looking for the _____ .

1.

B: The _____ ? It's on _____ Street. It's _____ .

2.   3.   4.

A: Thanks. And one more question. Where's the _____ ?

5.

B: Do you know the address?

A: Yes, it's _____ .

6.

B: Oh, that's _____ , on the _____ side of the street.

7.   8.

A: Thanks.

12 WHAT ABOUT YOU? **Answer the questions. Use your <u>own</u> words.**

1. "Where is your house or apartment?"

    YOU _____ .

2. "Where is your school?"

    YOU _____ .

LESSONS 3 AND 4

13 Look at the festival events listing. Then answer the questions. Use <u>in</u>, <u>on</u>, or <u>at</u>, if possible.

10th Annual Asian Folk Festival
Saturday, May 10 at the Park Arts Center in Rand Park
Events Listing

	Time	Location	Event	
	1:00 PM	Rand Park	Kite-Making Workshop	Children can make their own kite to fly in the park
	3:00 PM	The Park Arts Theater	Japanese Play: Children's Kabuki Group	Watch middle school students from Kobe, Japan perform a traditional play
	7:00 PM	The Rand Park Band Shell	Javanese Concert: Kiai Kanjeng Gamelan Orchestra	Hear music featuring drums, cymbals, and gongs from Java, Indonesia
	6:00 PM	The Rand Park Band Shell	Korean Dance: "Bu-che Chum" Fan Dance Troupe	See colorful dancers from Suwon, Korea perform a beautiful fan dance
	5:00 PM and 9:45 PM	The Park Arts Theater	Chinese Movie: *The Story of Lotus*	A love story set in the beautiful Wuyi mountains in Southern China

Plus try traditional Asian treats from China, Japan, Korea, and Indonesia. Food stalls will be open in the park from 12:00 to 8:00 PM.

1. When's the Asian Folk Festival? _____.

2. Where's the Japanese play? _____.

3. What time is the Javanese concert? _____.

4. Where's the Chinese movie? _____.

5. What event is at 6:00 p.m.? _____.

14 Complete the instant messages with information from the Asian Folk Festival listing.

Lara - Conversation 🔲🔳☒

File Edit Actions Tools Help

👥 Invite   🖼 Send Files   👁 Webcam   🎙 Audio   🚀 Launch Site

To: **Lara** Lara@email.com

Peter says: Hi, Lara. Are you free on [_____] ?
Lara says: Yes. Why?   **1.**
Peter says: The Asian Folk Festival is at the [_____] , in [_____] .
Lara says: What kind of festival?   **2.**   **3.**
Peter says: An Asian culture festival. Let's see . . . There's a Chinese movie, a Japanese [_____] ,
   a Korean [_____] , and a Javanese [_____] .   **4.**
      5.   **6.**
Lara says: Really? Sounds like fun! 😊
Peter says: I know you're a movie fan. Want to see the movie?
Lara says: OK. 👍 What time?
Peter says: There's an early show at [_____] and a late show at 9:45.
      7.
Lara says: Let's go to the early show—9:45 is past my bedtime! 😴

Read about the WOMAD festival. Then check ☑ <u>true</u>, <u>false</u>, or <u>no information</u>.

WOMAD festivals celebrate the international language of music.

The largest music festival in the world is WOMAD. WOMAD stands for World of Music, Arts, and Dance. The first WOMAD festival was in 1982, in Somerset, England. Since then, WOMAD has held more than 120 festivals in 21 countries. It has featured over 1,000 musicians, dancers, and artists from 90 different countries. Concert-goers hear rock, jazz, and folk music from all over the world, and go to workshops to learn about the music and instruments they hear.

SOURCE: www.womad.org

	true	false	no information
1. You can see a concert at the WOMAD festival.	☐	☐	☐
2. WOMAD is a classical music festival.	☐	☐	☐
3. WOMAD tickets cost $90.	☐	☐	☐
4. The musicians at WOMAD are from England.	☐	☐	☐

Write a short message to a friend. Invite your friend to an event. Use the Asian Folk Festival listing or your <u>own</u> event.

GRAMMAR BOOSTER

A ▸ **Complete the sentences. Write _in_, _on_, or _at_ on the line.**

1. There's a jazz concert ____ Tuesday.
2. The theater is ____ 10 Bank St.
3. My brother lives ____ Rome.
4. I finish work ____ 5:00.
5. I'm busy ____ the morning.
6. Germany is ____ Europe.
7. My house is ____ Carmel Road.
8. My parents married ____ 1970.

B ▸ **Choose the correct answer. Circle the letter.**

1. "Where's the play?"
   a. At The Grand Theater.   **b.** At 7:30.   **c.** In the evening.

2. "What time's the movie?"
   a. In March.   **b.** Tomorrow.   **c.** At 8:10.

3. "When's the concert?"
   a. On Tuesday.   **b.** On Ninth Avenue.   **c.** At my school.

4. "What time is class?"
   a. At night.   **b.** At 6:30.   **c.** At the bank.

5. "Where's his meeting?"
   a. On Tuesday.   **b.** At noon.   **c.** At 44 South Street.

6. "When's the art exhibit?"
   a. In November.   **b.** In the center of town.   **c.** At the City Museum.

7. "What time's the talk?"
   a. March 13.   **b.** Today.   **c.** At 1 p.m.

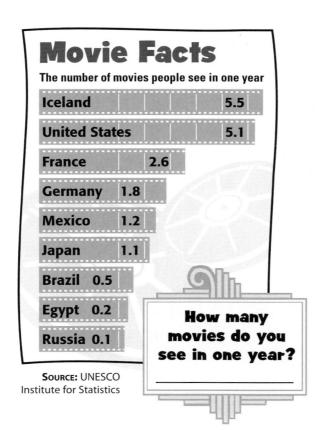

Movie Facts

The number of movies people see in one year

Iceland	5.5
United States	5.1
France	2.6
Germany	1.8
Mexico	1.2
Japan	1.1
Brazil	0.5
Egypt	0.2
Russia	0.1

SOURCE: UNESCO Institute for Statistics

How many movies do you see in one year?

_____

Complete the event listings with prepositions of time and place. Write _in_, _at_, or _on_.

Arts Week

VOL 1.

Band Plans Free Concert

The Swingtime Jazz Band's first free concert is **_at_** 8 PM ____
1.   2.

Monday. It's ____ Grand Hall ____ Wakefield Street ____ downtown
3.   4.   5.

Wellington. Call 999–555–8443 for more information.

Miracle Worker at Victoria University

Victoria University presents the play *The Miracle Worker* ____
6.

7:30 PM ____ Friday and Saturday, 4/23–4/24, and ____ 2:30 PM
7.   8.

____ April 25. The performances are ____ The Adam Concert Hall
9.   10.

____ Kelburn Road.
11.

Complete the conversations. Write questions with _When_, _Where_, or _What_. Complete the responses with a preposition.

1. **A:** _What time is the concert_ _____ ?

   B: I think the concert is _at_ 8:30.

2. **A:** _____ ?

   B: The play is ____ The Landry Theater.

3. **A:** _____ ?

   B: The supermarket is ____ Park Road.

4. **A:** _____ ?

   B: The exhibit is ____ January and February.

JUST FOR FUN

 Complete the crossword puzzle.

Across

4. film

6. artists' show

8. performance with actors

Down

1. not busy

2. music performance

3. not left

5. the spelling of 30

7. not good

BRAINTEASER. Who is a writer? A musician? An artist? An actor? Read the clues and complete the sentences.

A RIDDLE FOR YOU!

Question:
What's the number one musical instrument in the world?

Answer:
The human voice!

1. Ivan is an _____.

Clues:

Cleo's exhibit is at the City Gallery.

Paula is a rock guitarist with the group Jumbo.

Ivan is in a new play at the Cameo Theater.

Norman's talk is at Book World at 3:00.

2. Paula is a _____.

3. Cleo is an _____.

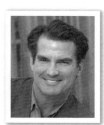

4. Norman is a _____.

Talking about Families

TOPIC PREVIEW

1 Complete the chart. Use words from the Student's Book.

Family Relationships		
Words for males	**Words for females**	**Words for males or females**
son	daughter	children

2 Complete the sentences with the correct family relationship.

1. My mother and my father are my _____.

2. My mother's father and my mother's mother are my _____.

3. My mother's brother's son is my _____.

4. My sister's _____ is my brother-in-law.

5. My brother's daughter is my _____.

6. My son and my daughter are my _____.

3 **CHALLENGE.** Look at the family tree website. Complete the sentences.

1. Rita is a _daughter-in-law_, a _wife_____, a _sister-in-law_, and a _mother_____.

2. Jane is a _____, a _____, a _____, and an _____.

3. Evan is a _____, a _____, a _____, and a _____.

4. Mark is a _____, a _____, a _____, and a _____.

Welcome to the Dalton Family Tree

You are visitor number: **1146**

Mary   Mark

Bill   Rita

Kim   Evan

Jane

Thank you for visiting our web page. Please sign our guestbook! CLICK HERE

LESSON 1

 Choose the correct response. Circle the letter.

1. "Tell me about your family."
   a. Not really.   **b.** Oh great!   **c.** OK, sure.

2. "Who are those people?"
   a. They're married.   **b.** They're my cousins.   **c.** Yes, they are.

3. "Do you have a large family?"
   a. No, they don't.   **b.** Yes, it does.   **c.** No, I don't.

4. "Does he have any brothers or sisters?"
   a. No, he doesn't.   **b.** He's an only child.   **c.** No, he isn't.

5. "Do you look like your mother?"
   a. Yes, I do.   **b.** No, she doesn't.   **c.** Really?

 Complete the paragraph. Use words from the box.

likes	doesn't like	works	has
live	work	doesn't have	lives

Juanita Diaz _____ in Puebla, Mexico.
1.

She _____ in a restaurant. She _____
2.   3.

Latin jazz, but she _____ rock music. She's not
4.

really a rock fan. She _____ any children, but
5.

she _____ two nieces and one nephew. They
6.

_____ in Tampico with Juanita's sister, Maria.
7.

Maria and her husband Roberto _____ in a school.
8.

 Choose the correct response to complete the conversation. Write the letter on the line.

A: Do you like Australia?

B: _____
   1.

A: That's too bad. Tell me about your family.

B: _____
   2.

A: Do you have a large family?

B: _____
   3.

A: Is your brother married?

B: _____
   4.

A: Does he live near your parents?

B: _____
   5.

a. No, he's single.

b. Yes, he does.

c. OK. What would you like to know?

d. No, I don't. I have one brother, but I don't have any sisters.

e. Yes, I do, but my family isn't here.

7 Look at the birth rate chart. Check ☑ true, false, or no information.

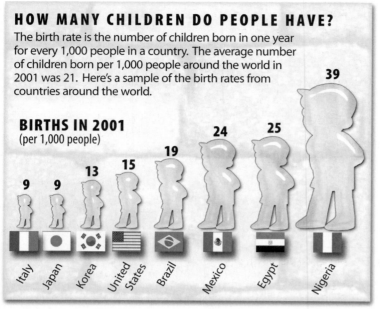

HOW MANY CHILDREN DO PEOPLE HAVE?

The birth rate is the number of children born in one year for every 1,000 people in a country. The average number of children born per 1,000 people around the world in 2001 was 21. Here's a sample of the birth rates from countries around the world.

BIRTHS IN 2001
(per 1,000 people)

Italy	Japan	Korea	United States	Brazil	Mexico	Egypt	Nigeria
9	9	13	15	19	24	25	39

SOURCE: www.worldbank.org

	true	false	no information
1. The birth rate in Mexico is 24.	☐	☐	☐
2. The average family in Japan has 9 children.	☐	☐	☐
3. The average birth rate around the world is 39.	☐	☐	☐

8 Look at the pictures. Write sentences.

1. _They're married_ . 2. _____ . 3. _____ . 4. _____ .

9 How old are people when they get married? Look at the chart.

Age at first marriage					
Country	China	Peru	Sweden	Tunisia	United States
Men	23	25	34	30	28
Women	22	23	31	26	26

SOURCE: United Nations Statistics Division

In these countries, are men or women older when they
get married? _____ .

10 Look at the responses. Write questions. Use words from each box.

Do Does	+	your daughter you your brother the manager your parents	+	like have work speak look live	+	like you? French? on King Street.? any photos of your family? on Saturdays? this music?

1. **A:** *Do your parents speak French* _____ ? **B:** Yes, they do.

2. **A:** _____ ? **B:** No, he doesn't.

3. **A:** _____ ? **B:** Yes, I think I do.

4. **A:** _____ ? **B:** No, she doesn't.

5. **A:** _____ ? **B:** Yes, she does.

11 WHAT ABOUT YOU? Answer the questions. Use your <u>own</u> words.

1. "Do you speak English with your family?"

   (YOU) _____ .

2. "Does your family have a website?"

   (YOU) _____ .

3. "Do you live near your parents?"

   (YOU) _____ .

LESSON 2

12 Complete the questions with <u>do</u> or <u>does</u>.

1. Where _____ George live?

2. What _____ your sister-in-law do?

3. When _____ you listen to music?

4. What time _____ your son go to school?

5. What _____ your friends call you?

6. How many sisters _____ you have?

How many people are there in the world? You can see a population clock on this website:

www.census.gov

13 Choose the correct response. Write the letter on the line.

1. ____ "What does Alex do?"

2. ____ "How many grandchildren do you have?"

3. ____ "Where does your mother live?"

4. ____ "What time do you go home?"

5. ____ "When do you visit your grandmother?"

6. ____ "What do you and your husband do?"

a. She lives with my sister in Madrid.

b. At 6:30.

c. He works at a bookstore.

d. I see her every July and December.

e. I have three.

f. We're both teachers.

14 ▸ **Look at the responses. Complete the questions.**

1. A: _What does_ Luigi _do_ ?
   B: He's a computer programmer.

2. A: _____ your cousins _____?
   B: They live in Hong Kong.

3. A: _____ your mother _____ you?
   B: She visits me every year in May.

4. A: _____ concert tickets _____?
   B: I only have two.

5. A: _____ to school?
   B: We go at 8:30.

6. A: _____ your younger brother _____?
   B: He looks like me. He's really cute!

15 ▸ **WHAT ABOUT YOU? Write a paragraph about someone in <u>your</u> family. Use the questions for ideas.**

- Where does he or she live and work?
- Who lives with him or her?
- What does he or she do?
- When do you see him or her?

(handwritten in margin: 2/3/11)

LESSONS 3 AND 4

16 ▸ **Read the article. Then answer the questions.**

Multiple births happen when more than one baby is born to the same woman at the same time. Twins are an example of a multiple birth; so are triplets (three babies born at the same time), quadruplets (four babies), and quintuplets (five babies). How common are they? In Australia, twins are born in about 1 out of 80 births, and triplets in about 1 out of 6,400 births. In the United States, twins are born in about 1 out of 33 births. Triplets are born in about 1 out of 585 births. In 2001, 1 out of about 47,000 births was quintuplets—or more!

Twins usually have the same birthday. But some twins are born on different days. And in late December 1999, some twins were born in two different centuries— one twin in 1999, and one in the year 2000!

1. Where are twins born in about 1 out of 33 births? _____.

2. What do you call three babies born at the same time? _____.

3. Do all twins have the same birthday? _____.

Look at the pictures. Check ✔ all the sentences that are true.

1. ☐ **a.** Mary and Ida both wear glasses.
   ☐ **b.** Mary wears glasses, but Ida doesn't.
   ☐ **c.** Mary wears glasses, and Ida does too.

2. ☐ **a.** Miki is a chef, but Jamie isn't.
   ☐ **b.** Miki isn't a chef, and Jamie isn't either.
   ☐ **c.** Miki is a chef, and Jamie is too.

3. ☐ **a.** Antonio speaks English, and Yoko does too.
   ☐ **b.** Antonio and Yoko both speak English.
   ☐ **c.** Antonio speaks English, but Yoko doesn't.

4. ☐ **a.** Jim is a jazz fan, but Thomas isn't.
   ☐ **b.** Jim isn't a jazz fan, and Thomas isn't either.
   ☐ **c.** Jim and Thomas are both jazz fans.

 Combine the sentences into one sentence. Use **but**, <u>both</u>, <u>too</u>, or <u>either</u>.

1. Jen likes rock concerts. Mark doesn't like rock concerts.

   Jen likes rock concerts, but Mark doesn't _____.

2. Chris likes coffee. Lola likes coffee.

   _____.

3. Joon is a new student. Kris isn't a new student.

   _____.

4. Mia doesn't have a large family. Greg doesn't have a large family.

   _____.

5. Jay looks like his father. His brother doesn't look like his father.

   _____.

CHALLENGE. Look at the sports website. Write a paragraph comparing the two famous athletes.

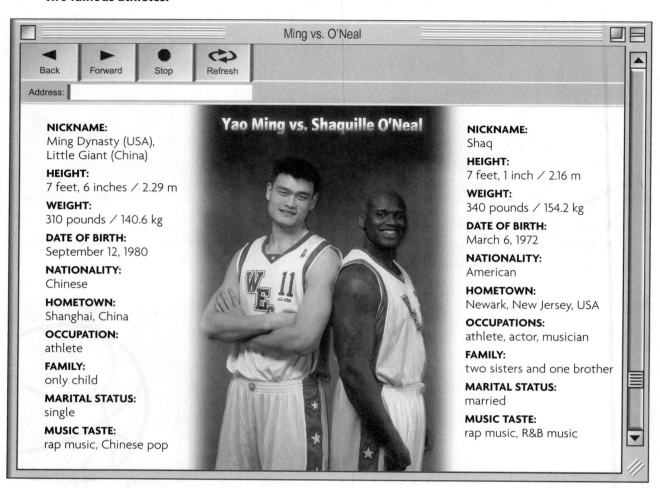

Ming vs. O'Neal

Back Forward Stop Refresh

Address:

Yao Ming vs. Shaquille O'Neal

NICKNAME:
Ming Dynasty (USA),
Little Giant (China)

HEIGHT:
7 feet, 6 inches / 2.29 m

WEIGHT:
310 pounds / 140.6 kg

DATE OF BIRTH:
September 12, 1980

NATIONALITY:
Chinese

HOMETOWN:
Shanghai, China

OCCUPATION:
athlete

FAMILY:
only child

MARITAL STATUS:
single

MUSIC TASTE:
rap music, Chinese pop

NICKNAME:
Shaq

HEIGHT:
7 feet, 1 inch / 2.16 m

WEIGHT:
340 pounds / 154.2 kg

DATE OF BIRTH:
March 6, 1972

NATIONALITY:
American

HOMETOWN:
Newark, New Jersey, USA

OCCUPATIONS:
athlete, actor, musician

FAMILY:
two sisters and one brother

MARITAL STATUS:
married

MUSIC TASTE:
rap music, R&B music

GRAMMAR BOOSTER

A Choose the correct response. Write the letter on the line.

1. _____ "Do you and your brothers play soccer together?"   a. Yes, we do.

2. _____ "Does your brother work in a restaurant?"   b. No, he doesn't.

3. _____ "Do your parents like music?"   c. No, I don't.

4. _____ "Does your aunt look like your mother?"   d. Yes, they do. Very much.

5. _____ "Do you live near here?"   e. No, she doesn't. She looks a

6. _____ "Do I need a tie?"   little like me.

          f. No, you don't.

B Complete the conversations. Write short answers to the questions.

1. **A:** Does he live in Sydney?

    B: _No, he doesn't_____. He lives in Melbourne.

2. **A:** Do your friends like Chinese food?

    B: _____. They go to Chinese restaurants all the time.

3. **A:** Do you have a big family?

    B: _____. I have eight brothers and sisters.

4. **A:** Does your husband work in an office?

    B: _____. He's a musician.

5. **A:** Do we need to buy our tickets now?

    B: _____. We can buy our tickets on the train.

C Complete the conversations. Write <u>yes</u> / <u>no</u> questions with the simple present tense.

1. **A:** He doesn't like concerts.

    B: _Does he like_____ movies?

2. **A:** My sister doesn't eat fish.

    B: _____ meat?

3. **A:** My grandfather doesn't drink tea.

    B: _____ coffee?

4. **A:** I don't like rap music.

    B: _____ jazz?

5. **A:** I have two brothers and one sister.

    B: _____ nieces and nephews?

D Choose the correct response. Circle the letter.

1. "Where do your grandparents live?"
   a. In São Paolo.   **b.** Yes, they do.   **c.** I don't think so.

2. "How often do you see your cousins?"
   a. In June.   **b.** Every month.   **c.** Yes, I do.

3. "When does he go to school?"
   a. In Mexico City.   **b.** In the morning.   **c.** No, he doesn't.

4. "Does your father eat meat?"
   a. No, he doesn't.   **b.** In the kitchen.   **c.** At 8 p.m.

5. "What time does your sister go to bed?"
   a. Yes, she does.   **b.** At midnight.   **c.** In the evening.

6. "How many people work in that office?"
   a. No, they don't.   **b.** Twenty or twenty-five.   **c.** I think so.

7. "Do Mark and Lisa speak Italian?"
   a. Yes, they do.   **b.** Yes, she does.   **c.** Italy.

E Look at the responses. Write information questions with the simple present tense.

1. **A:** *How many brothers and sisters does Anna have* _____?
   B: Anna? She has three brothers and one sister.

2. **A:** _____?
   B: Jon? He works in London.

3. **A:** _____?
   B: They usually start class at 8:00.

4. **A:** _____?
   B: Me? I like all kinds of music.

A Riddle for You!

Riddle: Two babies are born at the same time to the same mother, but they're not twins. What are they?

Answer: They're two of a set of triplets!

---

1 ▶ **Complete the puzzle. Write the letters of each word in the boxes.**

Across

1. your brother's son
2. almost the same
3. your mother's sister
4. not married

Down

5. brother-in-_____
6. aunt's or uncle's children
7. not older
8. mother and father
9. two children born at the same time
10. not the same

2 ▶ **BRAINTEASER. Who's who? Look at the family photos. Write the names under the pictures. Use the hints and the names in the list.**

Hints:

Shirley is Ted's grandmother.
Kelly is an only child.
Rick is married to Beth.
Cynthia has two nephews and one niece.
Mark and Barbara have two children.
Harry is Beth's father-in-law.
Cynthia is Barbara's sister.
Alex is Ted's older brother.

The Clark Family Tree

1. _____ 2. _____

3. _____ 4. _____ 5. _____ 6. _____ 7. _____

8. _____ 9. _____

10. _____

Names

Women	Men
Barbara	Alex
Beth	Harry
Cynthia	Mark
Kelly	Rick
Shirley	Ted

Coping with Technology

TOPIC PREVIEW

1 Look at the ads from a shopping catalog. Then check ☑ <u>true</u>, <u>false</u>, or <u>no information</u> based on the information given in the catalog.

ALL-STAR SPORTS WATCH

This tough digital watch is truly amazing! Perfect for playing sports, exercising, even swimming! It's waterproof to 1,000 meters. The large, easy to read display shows the day, month, and year. Only US$30! Order now!

Traveler 3000 Watch

Available here only! Do you travel often? Then the Traveler 3000 is the watch for you! Watch features two analog faces, so it's easy to see the time in two different time zones. Displays the day of the week. Your choice of silver, gold, or black face. Order yours today—only US$60!

	true	false	no information
1. The Traveler 3000 watch tells the day of the week.	☐	☐	☐
2. The All-Star Sports watch is a lemon.	☐	☐	☐
3. The Traveler 3000 watch costs US$3,000.	☐	☐	☐
4. Both watches tell the month and year.	☐	☐	☐

2 Take the survey about shopping catalogs.

What types of products do you buy from shopping catalogs?

- ☐ 1. Nothing. I like to shop in stores.
- ☐ 2. Clothes
- ☐ 3. Computer products
- ☐ 4. Electronic gadgets
- ☐ 5. Books
- ☐ 6. Music
- ☐ 7. Food
- ☐ 8. Movies
- ☐ 9. Other: _____

3 WHAT ABOUT YOU? Which gadgets or machines do you like? Which don't you like? Complete the chart.

Machines and gadgets I like	Machines and gadgets I don't like

LESSON 1

 4 Choose the correct response. Circle the letter.

1. "I'm looking for a new cell phone. Do you have any suggestions?"
   a. No, it's just a lemon.   **b.** Yes, it does.   **c.** How about a Global Mobile?

2. "What's wrong with your MP3 player?"
   a. It won't play.   **b.** It's expensive.   **c.** It's busy right now.

3. "What are you doing here?"
   a. I'm looking for a printer.   **b.** I'm not home right now.   **c.** It's printing.

4. "My laptop isn't working."
   a. It's terrific.   **b.** Any suggestions?   **c.** What's wrong with it?

 5 Complete each conversation with the present continuous.

What _is George doing_ here?
1. George / do

I think _____ for a new TV.
2. he / look

His TV _____.
3. not work

Yes, I am. _____ at 2:00.
5. I / leave

_____ to your
4. you / go
sister's house this weekend?

Who _____?
6. you / call

My brother-in-law. But his phone is busy.

I think _____ the Internet.
7. he / use

6 Read the questions. Write answers starting with <u>No</u>. Use the information in parentheses.

1. Is he leaving at 10:30? (11:00)

   <u>No, he isn't. He's leaving at 11:00</u> .

2. Are they studying for an exam? (look at a catalog)

   _____ .

3. Are you shopping for a laptop? (a PDA)

   _____ .

4. Is she going to the movie at 8:00? (7:30)

   _____ .

7 Write questions starting with <u>Is</u> or <u>Are</u>.

1. you / look for / a new computer

   <u>Are you looking for a new computer</u> ?

2. he / use / the computer / now

   _____ ?

3. they / buy / a CD burner

   _____ ?

4. Karla / work / today

   _____ ?

8 Look at the responses. Complete the questions. Use the present continuous.

1. **A:** What <u>are you looking for</u> ?

   B: I'm looking for a dictionary.

2. **A:** Who _____ ?

   B: Tom is going to the computer show.

3. **A:** What _____ ?

   B: I'm buying a new CD.

4. **A:** When _____ ?

   B: My sister is going to Vienna in June.

9 Look at Maria's PDA. Answer the questions about her schedule. Use the present continuous.

1. It's 12:15 p.m. What is Maria doing?

   _____.

2. It's 4:00 p.m. Is Maria going shopping?

   _____.

   What is she looking for?

   _____.

3. It's 9:15 p.m. Is Maria eating dinner?

   _____.

   What is she doing?

   _____.

| 10:00 AM |
| Call travel office |
| 11:30 AM |
| Call Dan about movie |
| 12:00 PM |
| Have lunch with Elias |
| 4:00 PM |
| Shopping; Look for DVD player |
| 7:00 - 8:30 PM |
| Have dinner with Mom and Dad |
| 9:00 PM |
| See movie with Dan |

10 WHAT ABOUT YOU? Answer the questions. Use your <u>own</u> words.

1. "Are you using a machine right now?" **YOU** _____.

2. "What are you doing tonight?" **YOU** _____.

3. "What about next weekend?" **YOU** _____.

LESSON 2

11 Complete the conversation. Use questions from the box.

| What's wrong with it?   How's it going?   Any suggestions?   What brand is it? |

A: Hi, Ed. _____
                          1.

B: OK, thanks. But my coffee maker's driving me crazy!

A: Not again! _____
                          2.

B: I don't know. It just isn't working. This thing is a piece of junk!

A: That's too bad. _____
                          3.

B: It's a Coffee Pal 300.

A: Sounds like you need a new coffee maker.

B: That's for sure. _____
                          4.

A: Well, how about a Brewtech? The model that I have is terrific!

B: Really? Thanks for the suggestion.

12 **Match the rooms on the left to the items on the right. Draw a line.**

1. bedroom   a. hair dryer, shaver

2. office   b. dishwasher, coffee maker, microwave oven

3. kitchen   c. computer, fax machine, copier

4. bathroom   d. TV, CD player, DVD player

5. living room   e. telephone, bed, TV

13 **Write each response in a different way.**

1. **A:** What's wrong?
   B: My printer won't print.

   _My printer's not working_____.

2. **A:** What do you think about Pell brand computers?
   B: Pell computers are great!

   _____!

3. **A:** My TV isn't working. I can't watch the big game tonight.
   B: I'm sorry to hear that.

   _____.

4. **A:** How's your new CD player?
   B: It's a piece of junk!

   _____!

14 **WHAT ABOUT YOU? Answer the questions. Use your own words.**

1. "Are you using any machines right now?"

   (YOU) _____.

2. "What machines do you use every day?"

   (YOU) _____.

3. "What machines do you never use? Why not?"

   (YOU) _____.

LESSONS 3 AND 4

15 **Look at the chart. Read the statements. Check ✔ true, false, or no information.**

Country	Cell phones*	Radios*	Personal computers*		true	false	no information
Brazil	25	403	48	1. Cell phones are not popular in Brazil.	☐	☐	☐
France	185	925	300	2. Personal computers are very popular in Portugal.	☐	☐	☐
Iceland	888	931	394				
Japan	503	949	315				
Portugal	305	299	104	3. 931 people have radios in Iceland.	☐	☐	☐
U.K.	728	1,414	338				
U.S.A.	247	2,049	574	4. Radios are expensive in the U.K.	☐	☐	☐
*per 1,000 people							

Source: CIA World Factbook, 2002

16 Look at the picture. Then complete the paragraph. Use the present continuous.

It's a busy Monday morning at the office of Techco Inc. The company president, Ms. Cline,

<u>is answering</u> her e-mail. She _____ tomorrow morning. She _____ to Brazil for a
    1. answer   **2. leave**   **3. go**

sales meeting. Her assistant, Frank, _____ on the phone right now. He _____ Ms.
                                          4. talk   **5. buy**

Cline's airplane tickets. Jim, a sales manager, _____ the photocopier and the fax machine.
                                                    6. use

He _____ copies of a report for the meeting and _____ a fax to Ms. Cline's hotel.
    7. make   **8. send**

Jeff and Aliza also work for Techco. They _____ the break room and _____ coffee.
                                              9. clean   **10. make**

17 Look at the picture. Find all of the problems in the office. Write a short
paragraph about the problems.

The employees at the Techco office are having problems . . .

_____

_____

_____

_____

_____

18 **Read the article about a famous electronic product.**

Presenting the Sony, er . . . Stowaway?

Mr. Akio Morita and Mr. Masaru Ibuka started the Sony Corporation in Tokyo in 1946. At first, Sony was a small electrical repair company. In 1953, they started to sell the first transistor radios. In 1979, Sony introduced one of their most famous products, the "Walkman" portable cassette player.

Sony engineers invented the Walkman after they noticed young Japanese people listening to music all day, even carrying large stereos to the park. They believed that people wanted a music player that was small enough to wear in a shirt pocket. Sony also wanted the cassette player to be easy to use, so that people could listen to music while doing other things like exercising, riding the train, or doing housework.

Sony Walkman™ Cassette Player

Sony chose the name "Walkman" for their new product. At first, the Walkman didn't sell well. Electronic stores didn't think people would buy it. Some thought that the Walkman would make people unfriendly and stop talking to other people. However, as more people heard about the Walkman, it became a big hit. Japanese music fans loved it. When Sony was ready to sell the Walkman in other countries, they worried that people would think that the name was bad English. They made plans to call it the "Soundabout" in the United States and the "Stowaway" in the United Kingdom. But Mr. Morita wanted his gadget to have the same name in every country, and today "Walkman" is its name all over the world. You can even find "walkman" in the dictionary! Since 1979, there have been 300 different Walkman models and over 150 million have been sold around the world. The Sony Walkman is now the best selling consumer electronics product ever made.

SOURCE: www.sony.net

Now read the article again. According to the information in the article, which adjectives describe the Sony Walkman?

☐ convenient
☐ guaranteed
☐ expensive
☐ fast
☐ portable
☐ popular

19 **WRITING. Do you think that the Walkman is a good product? Why or why not? Write a short paragraph.**

GRAMMAR BOOSTER

 A **Change each statement from the simple present tense to the present continuous. Use contractions.**

1. I eat breakfast every morning.

   I'm eating breakfast _____ now.

2. My mother buys a newspaper every day.

   _____ now.

3. They walk to school every day.

   _____ now.

4. It rains all the time in the summer.

   _____ now.

5. The bus stops in front of my house at 2 p.m.

   _____ now.

6. He runs in the park every afternoon.

   _____ now.

7. We close the store at 5 p.m.

   _____ now.

8. He writes the report on Fridays.

   _____ now.

B **Write negative statements. Use the words in parentheses.**

1. He's going to school now. _He's not working_ _____. (work)

2. Sonia and Lee are drinking water. _____. (tea)

3. Ted is writing a letter. _____. (do homework)

4. You're talking a lot. _____. (listen)

5. I'm reading a magazine. _____. (a book)

6. We're eating at my house. _____. (your house)

7. The fax machine is making a noise. _____. (print)

C **Choose the correct response. Write the letter on the line.**

1. _____ "Are you going to work now?"   a. A new coffee maker.

2. _____ "Is he studying for an English test?" b. No, he's not.

3. _____ "Where are you sitting?"   c. Next to Susana.

4. _____ "What is Tina buying?"   d. Yes, I am.

5. _____ "Are they listening to jazz?"   e. He's leaving in an hour.

6. _____ "When is he leaving work?"   f. Yuko and Miyumi.

7. _____ "Who's watching TV?"   g. No, they aren't. It's rap.

Write questions. Use the present continuous.

1. go / to the store / who

   Who is going to the store _____?

2. they / play soccer / where

   _____?

3. Sam / eat / what

   _____?

4. when / Lidia / come home

   _____?

5. my computer / why / use / you

   _____?

JUST FOR
FUN

1 ▷ **Look at the pictures. Write the words. Then look at the gray boxes ▢.**

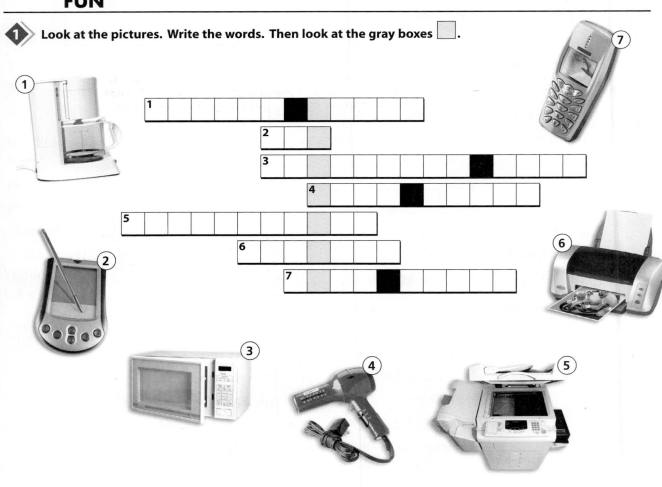

What's the new word? _____

2 **Read about the machines. Then write the name of the machine on the line.**

1. You use this machine to cook food and heat beverages fast. This first model is from 1947. It weighs over 750 pounds (340 kg). Today's models weigh just 25 pounds (11.3 kg)!

   What is it?

   a microwave oven

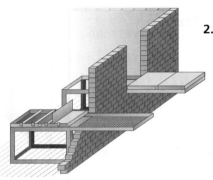

2. You can find this machine in almost every office. This model is from 1886. To use it, you open a window and put the machine outside. On a cloudy day, it takes one hour to make one copy! Today, these machines make hundreds of copies in seconds. And you don't have to open a window!

   What is it?

   _____

3. People use this machine on wet hair. This early model is from 1920. It is made of metal and is very heavy. It's not easy to use. Today's plastic models are light, easy to use, and portable.

   What is it?

   _____

4. This appliance is used to keep food cold. This 1916 model is called an "ice box," because you have to put big pieces of ice inside. Today's model has a different name, and you don't have to buy any ice!

   What is it?

   _____

You mean it's not a coffee cup holder?

Eating in, Eating out

TOPIC PREVIEW

1 Look at the menus. Then read the conversations. Where are the customers eating? Write the name of the restaurant on the line.

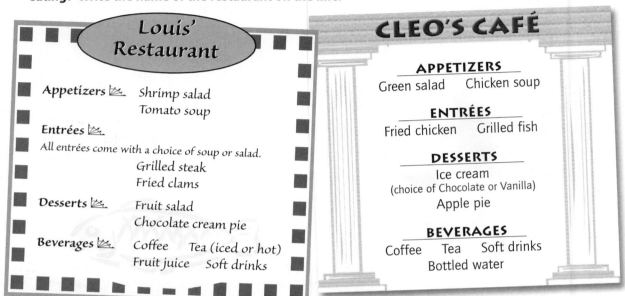

Louis' Restaurant

Appetizers 🥢 Shrimp salad
Tomato soup

Entrées 🥢
All entrées come with a choice of soup or salad.
Grilled steak
Fried clams

Desserts 🥢 Fruit salad
Chocolate cream pie

Beverages 🥢 Coffee Tea (iced or hot)
Fruit juice Soft drinks

CLEO'S CAFÉ

APPETIZERS
Green salad Chicken soup

ENTRÉES
Fried chicken Grilled fish

DESSERTS
Ice cream
(choice of Chocolate or Vanilla)
Apple pie

BEVERAGES
Coffee Tea Soft drinks
Bottled water

Are you ready to order?

Yes, thanks. I'll have the fried chicken.

Would you like to start with an appetizer?

Yes, I'd like a green salad.

1. _Cleo's Café_

2. _____

What comes with the entrées?

You have a choice of soup or salad.

Anything to drink?

Fruit juice, please.

3. _____

4. _____

WHAT ABOUT YOU? Look at the menus in Exercise 1 again. Where will <u>you</u> eat? What food will <u>you</u> order?

I'll eat at _____. I'll start with the _____.
Then I'll have the _____. I'll have _____ to drink,
and _____ for dessert.

LESSON 1

3 Complete the word webs. Write food categories and foods on the lines.

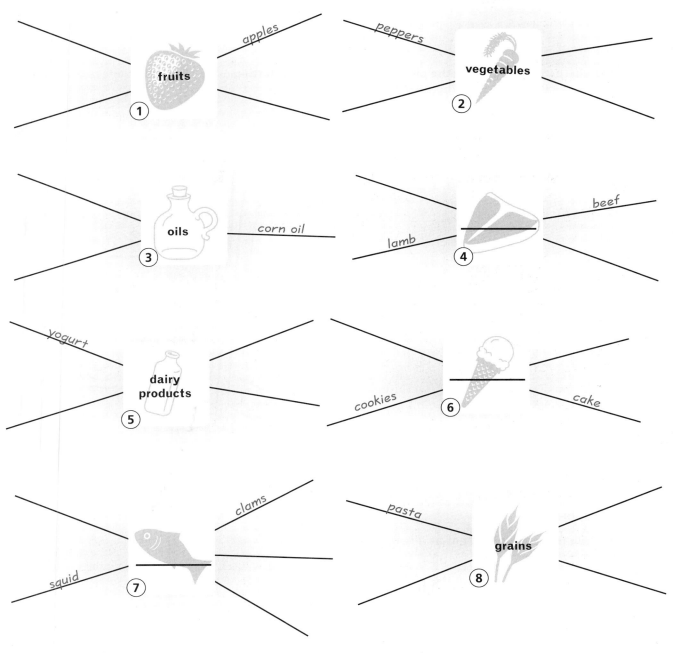

4 ▶ **Read the note. What foods does Nelson need? Write Nelson's shopping list.**

Hi Nelson,

Can you stop at the supermarket this evening?

We don't have anything to eat! There's no milk

and we're out of fruit. Can you get a chicken

and some vegetables (carrots, potatoes, peppers)?

We'll have chicken soup for dinner. I'm in the

mood to cook!

Thanks,

Kathy

Shopping List

5 ▶ **What's in the fridge? Look at the picture. Write sentences starting with <u>There is</u> / <u>There isn't</u> or <u>There are</u> / <u>There aren't</u>.**

Non-count nouns		Count nouns	
fish	lettuce	apple	carrot
sausage	juice	banana	orange
milk	broccoli	egg	onion
cheese	yogurt	grape	

6 ▶ **WHAT ABOUT YOU? Answer the questions. Use your <u>own</u> words.**

1. "What are you in the mood for right now?"

   YOU _____.

2. "What foods do you eat at a restaurant?"

   YOU _____.

3. "What foods do you eat at home?"

   YOU _____.

LESSON 2

7 Match the statement on the left with the explanation on the right. Draw a line.

1. " All entrées come with a choice of soup or salad. "

2. " The fried chicken comes with salad, doesn't it? "

3. " I'll start with the tomato soup. "

4. " Anything to drink? "

5. " I need some more time. "

6. " I'm in the mood for something spicy. "

a. The customer is asking about the menu.

b. The customer wants to eat something hot.

c. The waiter / waitress is taking a beverage order.

d. The customer is not ready to order.

e. The customer is ordering an appetizer.

f. The waiter / waitress is explaining the menu.

The first real restaurant with a menu with a choice of meals opened in 1765 in Paris.

8 Look at the responses. Complete the questions.

1. **A:** What _____ with?
   B: The bagels come with a choice of butter or cream cheese.

2. **A:** What _____ is there?
   B: There's white bread or wheat bread.

3. **A:** Anything _____?
   B: Coffee, please.

4. **A:** What _____ are there?
   B: Today we have ice cream, fruit salad, and apple pie.

9 Complete the conversations with **a**, **an**, or **the**.

Mary: Let's get _____ table.
1.

Joan: OK. Let's see. How about _____ table
2.
near the door? It's more convenient.

Mary: That sounds good.

Waitress: Are you ready to order?

Joan: Yes, we are. Do you have _____
3.
breakfast special?

Waitress: Yes, we do. We have _____ English
4.
Breakfast Special and _____ Continental
5.
Breakfast Special on _____ menu today.
6.

Joan: What does _____ Continental
7.
Breakfast Special come with?

Waitress: It comes with a choice of juice, tea,
or coffee and _____ basket of fresh-baked
8.
French bread.

Joan: I think I'll have _____ English Breakfast Special
9.
with coffee, please.

Mary: I'll have the same, but without _____ coffee. I'll have _____ glass of juice instead.
10.   11.

Waitress: Certainly.

The Sunrise Café

Breakfast Specials:
All specials include
your choice of coffee,
tea, or juice.

Continental Breakfast
Basket of fresh-baked
French bread

English Breakfast
Fried Eggs, Sausage,
Tomatoes,
Fried Potatoes

10 **WHAT ABOUT YOU?** **What food is in your kitchen? Complete the sentences.**
Use a or an if needed.

1. There is _____ in my fridge, but there isn't any _____.

2. There are _____ in my fridge, but there aren't any _____.

3. There is _____ in my kitchen, but there isn't any _____.

4. There are _____ in my kitchen, but there aren't any _____.

LESSONS 3 AND 4

 11 Look at the menu. Then answer the questions with short answers.

1. Does the pasta come with a salad?

   _Yes, it does_____.

2. What kind of soup is there?

   _____.

3. Is there any seafood on the menu?

   _____.

4. Are there any healthy foods on the menu?

   _____.

5. Is the fish entrée spicy?

   _____.

6. Does this restaurant accept credit cards?

   _____.

7. What kind of salad is there?

   _____.

JACK'S RESTAURANT

SOUPS
Clam Chowder   Chicken Vegetable

SALADS
Pasta Salad   Mixed Green Salad

ENTRÉES
ALL ENTRÉES INCLUDE A CHOICE OF SOUP OR SALAD.
Teriyaki Steak with mashed potatoes
Vegetable Beef Stew with carrots, potatoes, and peas
Pasta with tomato sauce
Grilled Fish with garlic and red pepper sauce

LITE ENTRÉES
Low-Fat Baked Chicken with cottage cheese and fresh fruit
Vegetable Sandwich—sweet bell peppers, cucumbers, carrots, and mixed salad greens on pita bread

BEVERAGES
Bottled Water   Soft Drinks   Tea   Coffee

= This is a hot dish!

SORRY, WE DO NOT ACCEPT CREDIT CARDS.

 12 Create a menu for the Healthy Choice Café. Write healthful foods that you like to eat under each menu category.

Healthy Choice Café
"EAT OUT WITH US AND EAT SMART!"

Appetizers
_Raw Veggie Platter_____

_____

Soups
_____

Entrées
_____

Desserts
_____

Beverages
_____

IMAGES: budgetstockphoto.com

GRAMMAR BOOSTER

 Complete the chart with nouns from the box.

~~rain~~	~~apple~~	cookie
water	fun	fish
fruit	cheese	bread
help	egg	onion

COUNT	NON-COUNT
apple	*rain*

B **WHAT ABOUT YOU?** Write <u>How much</u> or <u>How many</u> to complete the questions. Then answer each question using a countable quantity. Use your <u>own</u> words.

1. "_____ eggs do you buy each week?"

   YOU _____.

2. "_____ rain do you get in a year?"

   YOU _____.

3. "_____ fish is in your refrigerator?"

   YOU _____.

4. "_____ apples do you eat in a month?"

   YOU _____.

5. "_____ milk do you drink every week?"

   YOU _____.

C Complete the e-mail. Write <u>a</u> or <u>an</u> in front of count nouns or <u>X</u> in front of non-count nouns.

Brad,

I need __X__ help with dinner today. Can you go to the
   1.
store and buy _____ liter of milk and _____ loaf of bread?
              2.   3.
We also need _____ onion or two, and _____ kilo of apples.
            4.   5.
Do you think we have _____ cheese? If not, please get
                     6.
_____ package of that, too. I'll see you at home after 5:00.
   7.

Tracy

D Complete the conversations with <u>some</u> or <u>any</u>. For some items, more than one answer may be possible.

1. **A:** Do you need _____ bread?

   B: No, thanks. I have _____.

2. **A:** Do they want _____ soup?

   B: No, they don't want _____ right now.

3. **A:** I don't have _____ water and I'm so thirsty.

   B: Do you want _____ tea?

4. **A:** Does she need _____ help?

   B: She doesn't need _____ help. She needs _____ practice.

JUST FOR
FUN

1 ▶ **Read the sentences. Write the words. Then look at the gray boxes** ☐ **.**

1. You can have soup or a salad. It's your _____.

2. Eat foods from the _____ group in moderation.

3. It's not a good idea to eat a lot of _____ between meals.

4. Some people eat five or six small _____ a day.

5. Meat and cheese are _____ foods.

6. Fried foods and sweets can be _____ in fat and sugar.

1. | c | | | | | e |

2. | s | w | | | s |

3. | s | n | | | s |

4. | m | | | s |

5. | f | | | y |

6. | h | i | |

What's the new word? _____

2 ▶ **What is it? Write the word on the line.**

1. The waiter gives it to you at a restaurant. You read it to order food.
   It's a _____.

2. You eat them before your entrée. They are _____.

3. It's a healthy food group. Oranges and apples are in it. It's _____.

4. The waiter gives it to you after you eat. You can pay it with a credit card.
   It's the _____.

5. It's the amount of a food that you eat in one meal. It's a _____.

6. It's a very cold dessert. It's _____.

IMAGES: budgetstockphoto.com